AF531786

WOMEN IN THE PLAYS OF GEORGE BERNARD SHAW

By

Dr. Sangeeta Jain

Head
Department of English
Govt. P.G. College
Uttarkashi

DISCOVERY PUBLISHING HOUSE
NEW DELHI-110002

Reprinted - 2018

First Published - 2006

ISBN: 978-81-8356-047-4

Women in the Plays of George Bernard Shaw

Published by:

DISCOVERY PUBLISHING HOUSE PVT. LTD.

4383/4B, Ansari Road, Darya Ganj
New Delhi-110 002 (India)
Phone: +91-11-23279245, 43596064-65
Fax: +91-11-23253475
E-mail: discoverypublishinghouse@gmail.com
sales@discoverypublishinggroup.com
web: www.discoverypublishinggroup.com

Printed at:
Infinity Imaging Systems
Delhi

DEDICATED

TO

My Dear Mother

For Her Inspiration

Foreword

George Bernard Shaw-the name inspires a variety of reactions from scholars. Some love Shaw, some find him second to that great master of human emotions—Shakespeare, while others do not like him as they fail to grasp his tongue-in-cheek attitude and his philosophy of life, but students of literature have read him at some stage of their university education, nevertheless when Sangeeta came to me with a determination to work on Shaw, I was surprised. Today, when more and more scholars are trying to swim in the sea of Indian Writing in English, here was someone willing to work on a dramatist who tried to change the face of the Victorian Society in England and had succeeded.

Literature written at the turn-of-the-century, any century, is always of an exciting, thought-provoking and of diverse variety. Old order slowly, painfully dies out, new ideas germinate. The latter are received with mixed feelings. The last few decades of the nineteenth century were rich in all the literary modes markedly in the drama of the time. What is singularly significant about literature of this period is the interest in the female psychology and sexuality. Shaw's ideas were iconoclastic whether dealing with problems of love and marriage, war or martyrdom, prostitution or women at work place, and at the centre of each problem was a woman: fragile but determined, beautiful but powerful and consistently businesslike. She invariably emerged as a complex and central figure in the whole play. Shaw's women epitomize the manifestation of his unorthodox frame of mind which discredited the prevalent conventions and institutions regarding the status of women either in the society or at home. Candida in *Candida,* Louka in *Arms and the Man,* Barbara in *Major Barbara,* Ann Whitfieldin *Man And*

Superman, Vivie Warren in *Mrs. Warren's Profession*, Joan in *Saint Joan* Hypatia in *Misalliance* are some of the remarkable portrayals which have stayed with the readers of Shaw.

Shaw was forever keen to shock the society into thinking, and agreeing to a great extent, that women were not less intelligent than men but were only fundamentally different. His plays project his fight for the equality to women. Through such deliberations and thought-provoking discussions emerged *Women in the Plays of George Bernard Shaw* where the author, Dr. Sangeeta Jain, has projected Shaw as a writer much ahead of his times, thus proving his validity even today.

Meena Sodhi
Professor of English
Banaras Hindu University
Varanasi

Preface

Shaw's unorthodox and iconoclastic frame of mind is evident in the themes of his numerous plays where he subverted the conventional views on almost all the prevalent concepts of the society. Thus his treatment and presentation of women through whom he demonstrated his ideas, becomes an interesting and engrossing subject for any scholar of Shaw.

Women as a subject of literary writings have inspired many creative writers for a long time. This is especially the case in the twentieth century; as a result, the turn-of-century literature showed a great interest in the female personality and psychology. Women characters found in the drama of the first half of the twentieth century are varied and complex: from femme fatale to New Woman, from childlike waif to mature housewife, from hysteric to feminist, from barmaid to grande dame, from flapper to clotheshorse—women portrayals of diversified types have been depicted in different colours. The concept of "New Woman" was popularised with the advent of George Bernard Shaw, who upset and undermined traditional and customary mindset of the society. Shaw's unorthodox frame of mind and distrust of formulary attitudes and institutions as far as the status of women was concerned, both in the society as well as in the sanctuary of home, needs to be studied and re-evaluated today at the turn of another century.

This study presents an exploration of Shaw's notion of female protagonists, taking into account the masterly use of his personal involvement with many women of substance whom he encountered in his lifetime. Eleven of his plays are taken up as casestudy and some consideration is given, wherever appropriate, to other dramatic and non-dramatic writings of Shaw. A study has been made of the significant plays wherein women characters play an active role in the thematic concerns. *The Millionairess, The Heartbreak House, Back to Methuselah* have been included only partially because the women characters in the plays do not fit into any category nor is there any predominant female protagonist. Women characters in the plays are the central subject of discussion, keeping in view the then prevalent literary terms like "New Woman", "Emancipated Woman", "Intellectual Woman", "Avant-garde Woman" etc. However women characters have not been discussed on the basis of feminist critical theories.

Chapter I, "Emergence of Shaw and the Shavian Woman," traces the resurrection of the dramatic forms and places George Bernard Shaw as the pioneer of New Drama i.e. Drama of Ideas with the indelible and shaping influences of Robertson, Pinero, Henrik Ibsen, Karl Marx, Henry George, Nietzsche, Schopenhauer, Webbs; it shows how the Shavian forms differ from those of the early contemporary dramatists in England. This chapter presents the main outlines of "Shavian feminism" also with a critical account of the dramatist's views and concerns regarding the new generation of women. Shaw's theory of Life Force and its manifestation in the female characters of his various plays has also been incorporated.

Chapter II, "Women and Love," highlights multifarious shades and nuances of love—from amorous love to higher love and the mind blowing effect it exercises on women. Shaw has made his love-ridden women characters as agents of Life Force pursuing the better father for superhuman beings. In their pursuit of higher and better humans they shun the false sham and prudishness thrust upon them since centuries, making them mute dolls for the sake of social modesty. They represent independent women in love, women as subject choosing fearlessly the object of their love

Chapter III, "Women in Profession," foreshadows the plight of working women as they tend to feel intrinsic and extrinsic compulsions to take up cost-effective profession—from a helpless whore to adventurous acrobat—these professional women are representatives of different perspectives of professional life.

Chapter IV, "Women as Driving Force," comprises women or saviours who work for the welfare of society and its various man-made institutions like marriage, family, religion, with the significant unavoidable contribution made by them.

Chapter V, "Heroic Woman," has only one character, St. Joan forming the category of heroic and saintly woman. She epitomises the heroic spirit of woman with which a woman can reach sainthood and martyrdom.

The concluding chapter analysis various real life women and critics' statements about Bernard Shaw and his relation with women; finally it is discovered that Shaw worked for sexual equality and did whatever he could for women through the medium of drama—a very forceful form of entertainment at his time. The final remarks also pertain to our assessment of women in Shaw as a whole.

Author

Acknowledgements

It is with a deep sense of gratitude that I wish to thank all those who have helped and aided me in successfully completing my work on George Bernard Shaw.

I feel great pleasure in expressing my gratitude to Prof. Meena Sodhi, who consistently supported and guided me in my research work. She always reminded me of the need to study the material attentively.

I wish to acknowledge my gratitude to Prof. Vinod Bala Sharma, Delhi University; General Secretary, Shaw's Corner, Gurgaon for her invaluable suggestions and support. The library at Shaw's Corner was accessible to me and I could gather enough material for my work.

I am thankful to Prof. N.K. Lal, Head of the Department, Prof. M.K. Choudhary, Dean, Faculty of Arts, Prof. A.K. Tripathi, former Head, Prof. Sushila Singh, Prof. S.R. Jalote, for their suggestions and encouragement. My special reverence goes to Prof. R.S. Sharma for his advice. I pay special thanks to Dr. Asha Viswas for her guidance.

My obligations to Professor Isaac Sequeira, Director, ASRC, Hyderabad for giving his suggestions.

I acknowledge the assistance given by the librarian and the Assistant librarian, Mr. Vivekanand Jain and other staff of S.R. Gayekwad Library, B.H.U., J.N.U. Library, Central Library, Delhi University in the form of books and journals.

My mother, Mrs. Shashi Bala Jain has been a constant source of inspiration to me. This work could not have been possible without the ungrudging support of my father, brother, relatives and friends whenever I needed.

Sangeeta Jain

Contents

Introduction

Women as a subject of literary writings have inspired numerous creative writers for a long time. This is especially the case in the twentieth century writings; as a result the turn-of-the-century literature showed a great interest in the female personality and psychology. Women characters found in the drama of the first half of the twentieth century are varied and complex. From femme fatale to New Woman, from childlike waif to mature housewife, from hysteric to feminist, from barmaid to grande dame, from flapper to clotheshorse—women portrayals of diversified types have been depicted in different colours. "Change is the only constant thing in nature" is true to literature and literary theories as well. The concept of "New Woman" was popularised with the advent of George Bernard Shaw who subverted the conventional views on every aspect of the society. The present work has shown Shaw's unorthodox frame of mind and distrust of conventions and institutions as far as the status of women was concerned, both in the society as well as inside the sanctuary of home. The various chapters of the thesis have clubbed the different types of women from the wide spectrum of Shavian Panorama to form distinct categories.

The first chapter "Emergence of Shaw and the Shavian Woman" elaborates the re-emergence of drama in the twentieth century which did not decline in the nineteenth century but was transforming itself in response to significant cultural, social, economic and theatrical changes taking place. The steps towards literature were flourishing in the period. The contributions of T.W. Robertson, Henry Arthur Jones, Arthur Wing Pinero, Gilbert Wilde and Henrik Ibsen in the revival of drama and their influence on George Bernard Shaw has been discussed briefly in the first part. The second part highlights the emergence of George Bernard Shaw and the initiation of his writing career around 1880; this was the period when first feminist movement was in its infancy and was challenging the traditional concepts of woman as fundamentally different from and subordinate to man. Shaw supported the suffragist movement only through his writing and not as an activist. The concept of "New Woman" has been considered. As an ardent disciple of Ibsen, Shaw carried forward the "new race" of independent self-complacent woman projected through Nora Helmer in *A Doll's House* carving a niche by the importance and prominence of individual will of woman. Shaw's memorable and conspicuously strong, energetic female figures supplemented and championed the creation of the "New Woman" to exhibit that she is "a man in petticoats." Shaw's emotionally isolated relationship with his mother Lucinda Elizabeth Gurly, his platonic marriage with Charlotte and many cerebral affairs with prominent actresses and professional women taught him a lot about the psychology of women. Actresses like Ellen Terry, Mrs. Patrick Campbell, Florence Farr and socialist Beatrice Webb and many other associations with women helped Shaw formulate his views about the woman of substance, which he recast in his female protagonists. In different chapters, an attempt has been made to identify and elaborate all those prototype women whom Shaw preferred as role models to develop some of his great women characters. Shaw's theory of Life Force helped him in the portrayal of all women in his plays; these women have been shown to use this power for fulfilling different purposes in life.

The various chapters after the introduction have been classified and titled on the basis of the categories of women made by C.B. Purdom in *A Guide to the Plays of Bernard Shaw*. According to Purdom:

> "...the variety of Shaw's women characters is astonishing, all impelled by passion of one kind or another: from Blanche in *Widowers' Houses*, and Julia in *The Philanderer*, to Orinthia in *The Apple Cart*—there are abundant examples of the passion

of love, but as different from each other as women could be. Vivie in *Mrs. Warren's Profession*, Major Barbara, Lina in *Misalliance*,... and Saint Joan, represent another kind of passion, the passion for conscience, for work, for a cause, for God.... There are...other women such as Mrs. Warren,...Lady Britomart...[etc.] who belong to the world and Candida who belongs to herself. Such a gallery of remarkable women does not exist in the works of any other modern dramatist."

The second chapter entitled "Women and Love" highlights the multifarious shades of the emotions of the love-ridden women. Shaw has provided an open platform to the women in his plays to make their own choices of prospective mates without illusion and they choose fearlessly on the side of life. All these Shavian women rise in love not fall in love because they learn true love. Julia Craven in *The Philanderer*, Ann Whitefield in *Man and Superman*, Raina in *Arms and the Man*, Eliza Doolittle in *The Pygmalion* and Hypatia in *Misalliance* have been projected to have passionate love for their suitable paramour. Shaw adored and created these "agents of Life Force" because he believed that women had to be adored for the sake of the race, and love must be lifted on to the plane of consciousness for the sake of future.

The third chapter entitled "Women in Profession" portrays the Shavian career women confronting the catch-22 situation with the potential capacity to rise to the occasion. They are proactive, charismatic, energetic, self-made and self-driven. These women are loved and admired for their eminence in life not for insignificance like feminine selfless home birds. Mrs. Warren and Vivie in *Mrs. Warren's Profession* exemplify the helpless, unprotected but resilient and resolute women under the traumatic compulsion to work and to earn in order to assert their right to self. Lina in *Misalliance* is a superwoman and flapper leading an adventurous, complacent, self-opinionated life on her own terms. Louka in *Arms and The Man* is a headstrong social climber. In fact all these professional women work for a purpose larger than the self: the purpose being the re-awakening of the self-conscience of women and the proclamation of the Economic Independence.

The fourth chapter "Woman as Driving Force" focuses on the category of saving women. These saviours come to the rescue of society and to redeem the people. They take not only themselves forward but also their family and society. They make the society and its inhabitants learn the moral and ethical values and insufficiency, incompleteness of society without the substantial contribution of fully-independent women. Candida, Major Barbara, Lady Britomart and Grace represent significant types of evenly balanced and level-headed rescuers and redeemers.

Discussion on "Heroic Woman" forms the fifth chapter presenting a historical figure Saint Joan. It substantiates Joan, a country girl of seventeen, not as a sentimental heroine but as a heroic woman martyred for her faith and piety. She is the symbol of a "conflict between Private Judgment and Constitutional Authority." Joan, an unconventional female military leader and Saint has been portrayed as the precursor of Nationalism, Protestantism and female militarism. She is the perfect example of Shaw's androgynous mindset representing his philosophy of sexual equality.

The final chapter is the Conclusion in which we have gathered the main points of the thesis and on the basis of which we have determined that due to his puritanism Shaw could not easily combine the intellect and the body in his fictional women characters. Hence his women protagonists are endowed more with intellect and intellectual passion than with direct exterior sensuality and carnality. These women in Shaw's plays have provoked the critics down the years to pass judgment either in their favour or against them. One argument against these characters has been that they are untrue to life, invented merely for the stage, "born out of a union between Ibsen and Shaw in their well publicized elopement from Victorian sentiment." These stage inventions were taken as "untrue to life"; but Susanne Langer's theory on dramatic illusion projects drama as dealing with characters and events which will be valid in the future. Hence Shaw's women characters give us a glimpse of the women who were just like men as they would prove to be in the next century. Therefore while Shaw's contemporaries were creating heroines more and more womanly, Shaw was engrossed in creating women who were just like men, though they may be termed as "unsexed women." Shaw was busy designing women in the interest of political equality because he thought that a "man is a woman without petticoats." In his struggle and strife for equality he preferred women to govern in the interest of "national housekeeping."

1

Emergence of Shaw and the Shavian Woman

Nineteenth century drama is a "formless mass of mediocrity"; it is dull, repetitive, lacks literary quality and thematic significance. It is also a "vast sea of theatrical trivia and downright badness, a drama that slumbered fitfully for a hundred years while the glorious dawn of Shaw and Oscar Wilde waited in an East pregnant with momentous art."[1] This is the general opinion of literary historians and critics who thought nineteenth century dramatic and theatrical potential an arid wasteland of indifference and contempt.

It is true that drama, as an art form, did not reach to excellence for hundred years; yet its importance in imparting a concrete form to twentieth century drama cannot be dismissed absolutely. Capturing this invisible contribution of insignificant dramaturgy of nineteenth century, Michael Booth disagrees with the prevalent and run-of-the-mill opinion; he says "that drama did not so much 'decline' in the nineteenth century as transform its character in response to significant cultural, social, economic and theatrical changes."[2] It is not amazing and surprising that academic circles believe that English drama was reborn in the 1890s with the advent of William S. Gilbert, Arthur Wing Pinero, Henry Arthur Jones, Henrik Ibsen, George Bernard Shaw, Oscar Wilde, Granville Barker with Tom Robertson in the 1860s playing the pioneering role of an Apostle pointing to the light to come. An examination of the complex structure of the full-fledged drama from alpha to omega demonstrates the interwoven strands of early work comprising an essential part of the pattern of subsequent dramatic activity and its pre-eminence. It is evident that the playwrights of New Drama were indebted for most of their thematic material and style to previous generations of dramatists. Robertson, Pinero, Jones, Shaw and others imbibed food for thought from their ancestral dramatists hailing from Romantic and Victorian periods. Emphasizing this legacy inherited from earlier playwrights, Michael Booth writes:

> Shaw would not have written as he did, had he not been able to lay iconoclastic hands on the inherited wealth of Victorian melodrama and comedy, that Robertson's society comedies drew on Boucault's and Bulwar Lytton's before him...and so it goes with all the geners.[3]

This shows the omnipresent, ongoing change and development and not a complete break between old drama and new drama. New Drama was but old drama in new outfits—form and content, matter and manner. This also substantiates that drama did not diminish, rather the steps towards progression were slow and painful in the nineteenth century and had a phoenixian rise in the twentieth century as New Drama.

From Romantic and Victorian periods to Modern period, a revolutionary dramatical metamorphosis took place in the literary field. All the concepts inclusive of conventions, techniques, structure, character, purpose as well as dramatic perceptions were reversed. The change of dramatic rudiments from imaginary romanticism to reality of life transformed the whole scenario with realistic approach to theatre and drama. The theatre abandoned traditional modes of expression and came haltingly into modernity.

Theatre and drama both are inseparable from each other. Innovation and modification in one would lead to a drastic effect on the other. As the theatre developed, drama followed it and received new form. To understand New Drama, it is necessary to know the major developments in the theatre of the time. In and after 1800, the English theatre was a theatre of illusion and artificiality. Staging was symbolic, scenery with conventional designs of wood, castle, chamber, palace, and street, painted on the flat surfaces of wings and shutters that changed in grooves, moved on and off stage in full view of the audience, as it had since 1660. Players entered through proscenium doors opening and shutting upon library and forest alike. Acting, whether in tragedy, comedy, farce or melodrama, was considerably larger than life. It was artificial, stylized, energetic and highly emphatic. Enhancing the artificiality of character and acting Raymond Williams has remarked:

> The plays did not deal in nuances. Characters and action were drawn in bold theatrical lines: action was complicated and continuous in order to provide excitement and surprise and suspense in the theatre; characters, action were set in a single, simple, colourful mould, in order to provoke theatrical recognition.[4]

Dresses and costumes were old, suggestive of the period: sometimes traditional, sometimes exaggerated for comic effect, sometimes contemporary even in classical drama. Both the theatre and the auditorium were lit throughout the performance by candles and oil-lamps during the house-full event; pit and galleries were overcrowded. Audiences were made to sit on hard, backless, unreserved benches. It can be figured out easily that drama would be illusory when the theatrical conventions were so imaginary and unnatural.

By 1900 the theatre was a theatre of realism. The touch of reality was provided by staging, acting and costuming as well as all the other aspects of dramatic production. In place of built-up scenery, and elaborate imitation of the settings of modern and ancient life, there was the simple wing, shutter and groove system. The art of stage management and style of performance became more restrained and natural. For the first time theatre criticism was about underplaying and not overplaying. Costume and furnishings were exactly appropriate for a contemporary play. Well behaved audiences sat comfortably on reserved seats in darkened auditoriums, watching stages illuminated by the latest electric lighting. Michael Booth has explained the effect of theatrical reforms on drama:

> Thus traditionalism slowly broke down under the impact of changes in a theatre…that dramatic reforms would not have occurred without theatrical reforms preparing the way…the end of this road was reached before the twentieth century began….[5]

As the theatre became more modernised and drama more realistic, it attracted larger audiences from all around; the importance of the audience being very crucial in the evolution of drama. In fact the composition of the audience depended and changed according to decade, district, theatre, class and income level, housing, means of transportation to the theatre, and cultural tastes developing outside the auditorium. The population of London rose from nearly three million in 1850 to six and a half million in 1900, and the number of theatres also increased correspondingly. The spread of university education, the material prosperity, consciousness for social welfare gave an impetus to middle class public. The popularity and advancement of theatre in life and literary field are discussed in *Revels History of Drama in English*:

> The period 1880-1900 marks the birth of the theatre of the twentieth century as a social and literary force...radical changes came about...in the constitution and behaviour of its audiences. The theatre became fashionable, its artistes respectable; the breach between stage and literature was healed.[6]

It means greater literacy, scientific and technical progress, material prosperity all resulted in larger audiences who accepted theatre and theatre-people wholeheartedly. The theatre became an active force in the social life of the period.

The rise in the number of audience supported the elevation of the drama and dramatical reforms especially the contents of drama. The people were no longer interested in Romantic melodrama as they wanted something real. Observing this tendency to get more realism in audience, Michael Booth has written:

> As writing became less rhetorical and characterisation less extravagant settings and character types became socially more elevated...a ponderous realism immensely satisfying to audiences that hungered for even more realism and greater sensation.... The realism that aimed at an exact reproduction [of life]...[7]

The New Drama, the drama of serious artistic and realistic concern, began with T.W. Robertson (1829-1871). His work played a pivotal role in the transition and transformation of drama from

Victorian period to modern period. Not only the shape and significance of individual play but the feasibility of the technique employed in all the plays was also very considerable. His plays demonstrated innovative variations on conventional melodramatic structures which eased the existing tension between invention and convention caused by the change in theatre and society as well. As a founder of modern theatrical practices in England Robertson tried to adjust the scale and function of the visual side of drama imparting it greater realism of presentation. Hailing from a family involved with theatre business, Robertson knew how to change the whole environment. Focussing on Robertson's farsightedness Patricia D. Denison says:

> Having been involved with the theatre since boyhood days in his family's Lincoln based circuit theatre, Robertson was familiar with a tradition of theatricality that included both the actor/manager arrangement, which focussed attention on its leading actor and the stock company, which transferred its first repertoires of roles from one play to the next... [He] displayed his familiarity with a tradition that was soon to modify.[8]

As a playwright Robertson changed not only traditional theatrical conventions but social customs as well. He was eager to probe class-stratification rampant in society and the ramifications of rigid stereotyping. The two plays *Society* and *Caste* illustrate the importance of thematic intent in his plays and his emphasis on discussion rather than outright moralistic platitude. With the "cup-and-saucer drama" Robertson set out deliberately to introduce minute realistic observations of everyday life into the generally melodramatic, artificial theatre of 1860. Certainly he pioneered in imparting the theatre some of the broader issues (which get reflection in the title of the plays) through his plays *Society* (1865), *Caste* (1867), *Progress* (1869), *School* (1869), *Birth* (1870) and *War* (1871). These plays raised some controversial and conflicting issues, which paved the way for more realism in his successors. In all these plays he mixed new stage techniques with new social questions. Commenting on the novelty of Robertson, Patricia D. Denison thinks that he reconciled "revolutionary stagecraft with evolutionary social implications."[9]

Bernard Shaw praised Robertson's "tiny theatrical revolution." John Hare credited Robertson for founding a school of natural acting; it helped in completely revolutionising the then existing method. W.S. Gilbert lauded Robertson for inventing stage management, "an unknown art before his time."[10] Thus Robertson provided models for turn-of-the-century playwright and producers by giving stagecraft and explosive social themes. Expressing the significance of Robertson's contribution, Gassner has observed that:

> ...Robertson brought into the theatre a new realism and it is for this reason that plays like *Caste* and *Society* can be called "modern plays" and Robertson himself designated as one of the important pioneers in the sire of the new drama.[11]

Drama started reflecting a growing concern with the essentials leaving behind the superficialities of life. Jones, Pinero, Gilbert, Wilde and even Shaw, were Robertson's real heirs as their interests had striking similarities with those of Robertson. Henry Arthur Jones (1851-1929) and Arthur Wing Pinero (1855-1934) were trying their hand at thesis drama with themes of social significance. Jones insisted in presenting the drama something more valuable than mere entertainment and recreation, portraying all the shades and nuances of passions in human life. He fought for largeness and breadth of view against the cramping and deadening influences of pessimistic realism. He wrote some serious plays—*Saints and Sinners* (1884), *Judah* (1890), *The Masqueraders* (1894) apart from melodramas and comedies of manners. In his plays Jones provided realism and new techniques of dramatic construction in an intermingled way. On this synthesis in Jones plays the comment in *Revels History of Drama in English* is to be noted that Jones was successful in achieving "a workable modern play or, to put it another way, a fully fledged English well made play,... [mixing] methodical construction learnt from the French with Robertsonian realism."[12]

Arthur Wing Pinero, with the solid foundation of the cup and saucer" realism of Robertson, with the well-made dramatic construction of Scribe and other French writers and problem plays of Ibsen, got popularity through his series of farces written for the court theatre—*The Magistrate* (1885), *The School Mistress* (1886) etc.

He got his real place with his plays which presented conflicts and clashes between society and its characters. *The Profligate* (1889), *The Notorious Mrs Ebbsmith* (1895), *Iris* (1901) and the most famous *The Second Mrs. Tanquery* (1893). Pinero's characterisation of women set him apart from his contemporaries. His galaxy of women characters comprising Agatha and Charlotte (*The Magistrate*) Georgiana Tidd (*Dandy Dick*) and Lady Castle Jordan (*The Amazons*) are excellently drawn. Beryl, Paula, Agnes and soppy Mrs. Ebbsmith establish his superiority in characterisation of feminine characters. But he lacked one thing i.e. he could not break the shackles of traditions regarding women. For his brilliant characterisation and shifted play-construction Pinero was superb but he lacked vision, "the breadth of view of Jones, the reformative drive of Shaw, and the philosophical outlook of Ibsen."[13]

Of all the dramatists, Robertson, Jones, Pinero the most influential was Henrik Ibsen (1828-1906). Ibsen was never interpreted positively until Shaw endorsed his ideas and ideals presenting rhyme and reason behind them. With the London performance of *A Doll's House* (1889) and of *Ghosts* (1882) and *Hedda Gabler* (1891), Ibsen was criticised and abused by majority of critics and the so-called moralists. Clement Scott criticized Ibsen harshly in an article in *Daily Telegraph* centring round his own review of Ghosts. He wrote:

> ...this so called master...who is to teach the hitherto fairly decent genius of the modern English stage a better and a darker way, seems, to our judgement, to resemble one of his own Norwegian ravens emerging from the rocks with an insatiable appetite for decayed flesh.[14]

Ghosts was compared to "on open drain; a loathsome sore unbandaged; a dirty act done publicly; a lazar-house with all its doors and windows open."[15].

For Ibsen there were many face-savers and defenders. Shaw, one of the most vehement and vigorous of supporters, turned the table in his favour. He presented Ibsen as a moral leader and a great teacher who taught the lessons of giving importance to individual will and in the exploration of individual will's independence there would be the emergence of social conflicts. Ibsen taught that without struggle and conflicts between society and an individual there is no progression. Shaw wrote *The Quintessence of Ibsenism* (1891) "an exposition of Ibsenism"[16] (as he himself called it) and cleared the way for him to get into the social structures against rebellious outcry. Writing about the importance of Ibsenite guidance Shaw says:

> Nobody now dreams of calling me a "muck ferreting dog" because I think Ibsen a great teacher.... It really matters very little whether Ibsen was a great man or not: what does matter is his message and the need of it.[17]

Without Ibsen it would be difficult to understand scriptures and high moralists.

> It is not too much to say that the works of Ibsen furnish one of the best modern keys to the prophesies of scripture. Read the prophets, major and minor, from Isaiah to Malachi, without such a key; and you will be puzzled and bored by the almost continuous protest against and denunciation of idolatry and prostitution.[18]

Ibsen's reputation as the greatest revolutionary dramatist of the nineteenth century rested on his last plays, termed as "objective anti-idealist plays." *The League of Youth* (1869), *Pillars of Society* (1978), *A Doll's House* (1879), *Ghosts* (1882) and *An Enemy of the People* (1882) are some of the most popular plays which exercised a great and lasting influence on English dramatists. These plays were Ibsen's main contribution towards the growth of the "Problem play" in England. The subject matter of these plays presented a very realistic criticism of society. Ibsen criticized the sham respectability, commercial political ideals and attacked the institutions of marriage, degenerated morals and Victorian code of conduct. He gave greater emphasis to the individual will. Commenting on Ibsen's psychology of giving importance to natural will, Raymond Williams has observed that "...Ibsen was an artist, for whom the communication of significant experience must be the primary concern.... There is a certain thematic element of "Vocation" an experience to which Ibsen was to return again and again: the essence of freedom is to fulfil our call absolutely."[19] The persistent theme of Ibsen's plays was the contrast between the "actual and the ideal," "Man against men"; "the individual" against "society"... The vocation is liberation; the realisation of what "man can become."[20] Thus, Ibsen while emphasising the ordinary and subtle details of life in the naturalistic fashion, insisted on realism on the stage.

"Modernism" starts with this new way of thought launched by Ibsen and his followers, Strindberg, Hauptmann, Sundermann were other naturalist representative writers in the European Countries who were on the same wavelength with Ibsen. Explaining the concept of modernism, Robert W. Corrigan says:

> Modernism involves both the conviction and practice that to be modern is to be, in many important ways, different from anyone who ever lived before. This does not mean that man has changed; human nature is the same, but man's way of looking at himself has changed in a way that is significantly new. It is this new view of man that creates the problem for the dramatist.[21]

Bernard Shaw was greatly influenced by Ibsen and his contemporaries. Taking this new view of man and society Shaw created a new drama with social issues which became the acceptable parameters for the British theatre. Christopher Innes thinks that Shaw initiated the new wave and says that:

> Picking up Ibsen's brand of Naturalism, which he [Shaw] reinterpreted to form the basis of a rational drama dealing with the social issues, Shaw defined modernism in a way that became standard for mainstream British theatre.... It is largely due to Shaw that British Drama in the twentieth century is distinct from the European tradition, rather being the effect of cultural, or even linguistic differences.[22]

Shaw entered the theatre when the high and elevated styles of Ibsenite realism in modern outfits and Greek ritualism were challenging the domination of Shakespearean and Victorian traditions in the theatre field. This realist revolution was further fanned by Bernard Shaw. At the very outset, Shaw had to prepare the grounds for himself and his reformative and humorous plays because the puritanic attitude and pressures were still prevalent in the society as well as in theatre. Commenting on this struggle between Shaw's hilariousness and social puritanism, Margery M. Morgan writes:

> He had to fight his chosen enemies within himself as well as in society, and the battle proceeds on other levels besides the rational. Under the extreme pressures of puritan tradition in morals and manners, humour may be both personally liberating and socially subversive in a gradual and insidious fashion.[23]

As a dedicated socialist, an active public speaker and a pamphleteer for the cause of realistic drama, Shaw's foremost objective behind the drama was the reformation of society through imaginative thinking and scientific reasoning. These two traits are entirely opposite to each other yet Shaw combined them successfully. On this combination and amalgamation of two contradictory things Margery M. Morgan has observed:

> Imaginative thinking, thinking through the medium of art, is a different activity from scientific reasoning or the mode of argument followed by a political orator, educator or polemicist. The two types of activities seem to have been complementary to each other in Shaw's life: the one didactic and directive, the other turning inward with a self-searching regard as much as outward in communication with others.[24]

Shaw's contribution to serious drama in both matter and manner is unquestionable. He always insisted that dramatic writing was an art and not a craft. The theatre being always a means to an end with him and the end itself being not artistic but sociological. In fact theatre was a fully flourishing industry when Shaw emerged and this availability of important theatres or the playhouses helped Shaw in realising his dream of writing the socialistic drama. Shaw and his contemporaries were successful because there were J.T. Grien's Independent Theatre, the Stage Society and the J.E. Vedrenne-Granville-Barker Court Theatre (1904-1907) for the production of their plays. Without such organisations undoubtedly the way for the New Drama would not have been prepared.[25]

Shaw was not completely under the impression of the concept of well-made play adopted by Robertson, Pinero and Jones because he thought the play was more than a compact, contrived thing. He wrote in *The Quintessence of Ibsenism* that in a well-made play, there is an exposition in the first act, in the second act a situation and in the third disentangling of the situation. But now there would be exposition, situation and discussion; and the discussion is the "text" of the playwright; Shaw never looked at drama as "formula" but a chance for the "exchange of ideas."[26] Shaw revolted against the well-made play because it gave undue emphasis on the plot and not on characters and theme. He thought that "in this dramaturgy the Aristotelian doctrine of the primacy of plot had been driven to an improper extreme. The plot was now, not primus inter pares, but all that mattered."[27] There was no organic relation between plot character and theme. So it became an aversion to the advocates of New Drama at the Century's close. He never adopted the well-made play in a strictly conventional style with a plot determined play and stereotyped characters. He produced more active characters and their decisions affected the course of events. He had the impressions of well-made play somewhere at the back of his mind but he utilized them in his idiosyncratic way. Commenting on Shaw's use of well-made play technique to suit his purpose, Eric Bentley has observed, "Of Shaw's 'Play-making' one must conclude that he knew how to put together a Scribean plot; that he knew how to subordinate such a plot to his own purpose."[28]

Advancing from artificiality and superficiality inherent in the late Victorian drama to realistic and naturalistic drama, Shaw established and accelerated the problem plays. He raised different economic, religious, social and political questions in his plays. His plays of the nineties and the first decade of the twentieth century certainly demonstrate this concern for socio-economic conflicts of society. *Widowers' Houses* (1892) deals with slum landlordism and the so-called pleasant people who are not at all interested in the original source of their money. *Mrs. Warren's Profession* (written 1893; published 1898) raises the same question of tainted money through the means of prostitution. *The Philanderer* (written 1893; published 1898) deals with newly discovered concept of "New Woman". All these three plays were Shavian variations of the problem play. In *Arms and the Man* (1894) Shaw satirizes the military and exposes the futility of war and higher love. In *Candida* (1895) he deals with the reality of marital relations. *The Devils Disciple* (1897) gives an indepth analysis of marriage, war and heroism. In *Pygmalion* (1913)

Shaw comments on caste and class snobbery. *Man and Superman* (1905), the most philosophical play, deals with the ultimate aim of creative evolution. Drama definitely was more than a genre to Shaw through which he tried to change the sham ideals of society. Shaw wrote in *The Quintessence of Ibsenism*:

> In the new plays the drama arises through a conflict of unsettled ideals rather than through vulgar attachments, rapacities generosities, resentments, ambitions, misunderstandings, oddities and so forth as to which no moral question is raised.[29]

No heroes, no villains, no right, no wrong but a real problem discussed at length. Human and social problems became the source material of naturalistic plays written by Bernard Shaw.

The feminine consciousness was raised by many movements to liberate and encourage women to take initiatives and come out from the long oppressed womanhood. This state of affairs is expressed in the following lines:

> Saw the infants doomed to suffering,
>
> Saw the maidens slaves to lust,
>
> Saw the starving mothers barter,
>
> Souls and bodies for a crust,
>
> Then she rose—with inward vision,
>
> Nerving all her powers for good;
>
> Feeling one with suffering sisters
>
> In perfected Womanhood.[30]

Two early crusaders for women's rights were Mary Wallstonecroft and John Stuart Mill. Mary Wallstonecroft projected her bold and startingly new ideas and concepts in *Vindication of the Rights of Woman* (1792). She wrote it in response to a program in France during the revolution that denied girls schooling after the age of eight. Commenting on the book Showalter said that Mary, "anticipated virtually all the demands of the woman's movements—education, legal representation, the right to vote, the right to property and admission to professions."[31] John Stuart Mill's *Subjection of*

Women (1869), often called "the feminist Bible," created a lot of controversy and antagonism. However, he thought that his intention in writing the book was for the general development of the society and the individual's liberty. His sympathy towards feminism was one aspect of his conviction of an individual's liberty. He stated that women's position was not natural but was the result of political oppression by men. Elaborating Mill's idea, Gail Finney reflects that:

> Mill's *Subjection of Women* (1869) deplores the fact that women have been socially conditioned to live for others and deny themselves, to shut themselves off from productive occupations, and, worst of all, to assent in their own subjection.[32]

This shows that the widely used term "feminism" is a new term for the same old thought which had its seed and origin in the eighteenth and nineteenth centuries. But the term "feminism" came into being in 1895.[33] This was the time when Bernard Shaw was an u coming dramatist and a social worker.

Shaw was under the influence of Buffon, Lamarck, Butler, Schopenhaur, Bergson, Nietzsche, and Marx, Henry George and many others. He described himself as the spokesperson of the Webbs—the Pioneers of British socialism, whose ideas he propagated as a Fabian socialist. Does it mean that he took the role of a feminist through reforming the society? Before answering this question we will explore the connection between feminism and Shaw.

Elaine Showalter's *A Literature of their own: British Women Novelists from Bronte to Lessing* (1977) traces the history of women's writing through three phases—the "feminine" from 1840-80, the "feminist" from 1880-1920 and the "female" from 1920 onwards.[34] The feminine phase was the period when women used to write under male pseudonym as the Victorian society put curbs on women. In the feminist phase, women suffragettes were struggling to acquire the right to vote and ultimately they won it and the third phase, i.e., Female phase was the phase of self discovery, a search for identity. It is in the second phase, the feminist phase, when there was the protest against the imitation of the prevailing modes of the dominant tradition, and internalisation of its standards of art and its views on social roles with advocacy of minority rights and values, including a demand for autonomy that Bernard Shaw was moving towards the zenith of his achievement. Although women's liberation, feminist movement, women's lib were the terms that drew attention as a forceful and influential struggle in the 1960s, Shaw, through his writings and creation of women characters, forestalled it in the beginning of the twentieth century.

What is "feminism" and how can Barnard Shaw be associated with this ideology? "Feminism" is a theoretical and literary term with historical, sociological, political, psychological connotations. Commenting on the extensiveness of feminism, Gail Finney defines it "as a historical or sociological term [which] refers to the drive for equal rights for the sexes."[35] Showalter defines it "the feminists' protest [against]—legal, economic and social restrictions on the basic rights of women…"[36] Bernard Shaw, in the early twentieth century, pioneered and advocated similar ideas. He vehemently supported the notion of equality for both men and women. The period 1880-1900 was the time when the First Feminist Movement was in its infancy and challenging the traditional view of conceptualising and thus condescending women as fundamentally different from and subordinate to men. The responses of women to the conventional inferiority of their sex were of double spectrum—feminism and hysteria. Freud's was one of the most emphatic voices at turn-of-the-century patriarchal society. Freud described hysterization as internal emancipation of female. External emancipation resulted in feminist movements.[37] The turn-of-the-century drama was affected by these two diverse theories and the corollary was the section of strikingly diverse female figures. European theatre goers were treated to Synge's Pegeen Nike, Strindberg's Laura and Miss Julie, Wilde's Salome, Ibsen's Nora Helmer and Hedda Gabler, Wedekind's Lulu, each representative of its own class and individualities.

Bernard Shaw also created memorable and conspicuous female figures in his play which resulted in the creation of the "New Woman." Gareth Griffith is of the opinion that:

> By the 1890 Shaw's name was connected intimately with the propaganda on behalf of 'the new woman.' As the

> arch progressive he was eager to argue the case for radical feminism, to preach the rebel's gospel of liberalism.[38]

What was the concept of the New Woman and how did it originate? What were the chief characteristics of the New Woman? Was it reality or a mere myth?

Women started striving hard in order to be recognised as a human being and not as a commodity. They began hunting for jobs and careers outside their homes. There was a sudden change in the outlook of women towards themselves and society. Capturing this transformation of women's ideas about themselves, critics and journalists coined the term "New Woman" which reflected a diversion from self-sacrificing old woman. Explaining this origin of the concept of "New Woman", Gail Finney writes that she was:

> A product of combined forces—notably the drive for female suffrage, the influx of women into factory jobs and other kinds of work, and the example of Ibsen's heroines-the New Woman was less a reality than a creation of Fiction and the media.[39]

The influence of Ibsen's women characters would be dealt extensively in the subsequent part of the chapter. On the creation of New Woman Carolyn Forrey observes:

> Journalists seized hold of the term in the 1890s to try to describe the changes which they sensed were taking place among women; changes not so much in women's outward movements as in their outlooks and expectations.[40]

The crucial factor of the typical New Woman which differentiated her from the old woman was her rebellious attitude towards subservient "old woman" who was described by one member of 1890s women's club as "bounded on the north by servants, on the south by children, on the east by ailments and on the west by clothes."[41] Unlike conventional Victorian woman, the New Woman was not accustomed to self sacrifice; she chose her career for a living and pursued self fulfilment and independence. She strove for equality in her relationships with men, discarding the double standard of sexual mores of the time and was much more frank about physical relationships. Sometimes she selected living single instead of getting entangled in the illusions of married life. She was well-educated and an omnivorous reader, much interested in business and politics. She was physically well-built and energetic, preferring comfortable clothes than voluminous dresses of the Victorian woman. She could smoke, fly planes, ride bicycle, had short hair: all of which were considered to be quite daring at that time. This hybrid combination of New Woman mushroomed in the late nineties literature; but she met fatal ends reflecting that the society was yet not ready to accommodate her. Many of these characteristics formed the features of Shaw's creation of women except the last one that Shaw's women were winners and not losers. He was the first to bring the New Woman on the stage who won what she desired.

In the formation of the New Woman, Henrik Ibsen's contribution is of paramount importance. As a matter of fact, Henrik Ibsen was an unconscious, unassuming pioneer of the feminist cause. Although Ibsen never envisaged himself as a champion of woman's rights yet intentionally or unintentionally he strongly supported woman's cause in his plays as well as in personal life. While addressing the Norwegian Women's Rights league in 1898, Ibsen refused the honour of being a leader and a supporter of women's liberation by saying:

> I must disclaim the honour of having consciously worked for the emancipation of women. I am not, infact, entirely sure what women's emancipation really is; my concern has been with the emancipation of people.[42]

Making an emotive speech in 1879, to the members of Scandinavian society in Rome, Ibsen directly requested women's recruitment for the post of librarian and franchise for them. He was fiercely opposed and was so much outraged at the opposition that he stopped visiting the society for sometime.[43] In 1884 he with other authors demanded the legal authority for married woman. He stressed that both man and woman should enter the institution of marriage with equal legal rights.[44]

Ibsen was inspired by the Norwegian pioneers of the feminist movement like Camila Collet (1813-1895), Norway's first feminist author and first realistic novelist in Norwegian literature, and Aasta Hansteen (1824-1908), an accomplished portrait painter, who abandoned that career in favour of working for women's cause. Ibsen learnt most of his authoritative feminist stand from these two feminists. They also believed, like Ibsen, that laws should be written again in order to provide greater protection and security to women. They also thought that legal rights alone were not sufficient to provide individual freedom, there should be something on the moral and spiritual level. Katherine Hanson writes about them:

> In their writings these women advocated a spiritual emancipation; they demanded greater respect for women as women, for feminine abilities, feminine emotions—in a word, for the feminine personality.[45]

As a corollary to these feminist enthusiasts' cry for liberty, emancipation and equality, Ibsen penned his extremely radical feminist play *A Doll's House* published in 1879. This play aroused a furore among the ranks of bourgeoisie throughout Europe. Nora was the first female character of Ibsen whom the public took as a living woman of flesh and blood. She was discussed as a real woman and not fictional. In a series of articles published in 1884 in "Luthersk Ugeskrift" Pastor M.J. Faerdan warned his parishioners to be alert regarding the new, emancipated women:

> Just as Nora appears in the final scene, free and unfettered by any bond, divine or human, without commitment or obligation the man whom she has given her promise or to the children she has brought into this world—like wise we will find the wife in the modern marriage, from beginning to end. In the future her place will not be in the innermost sanctuary of the home, like a priestess at its hearth and altar. The emancipated woman has taken her place at the door, always ready to depart, with her suitcase in her hand. The suitcase—and not, as before, the ring of fidelity—will be the symbol of her role in marriage.[46]

This description shows the terror engendered by Nora; thus the New Woman was supposed to have discarded all the traditional norms and beliefs of sticking to her family. Despite all the atrocities of men, she was inclined to observe fidelity but Nora rebelled against it and framed the way outside the home for women folk.

Gina Krog (1847-1916) was a leading figure in the women's movement in Norway, beginning in the 1880s and one of the founders of the Norwegian Women's Rights League. As the first editor of "Nylaende," a feminist journal published from 1887 to 1927, in an article on *A Doll's House*, she anticipated that the book was indication of a terrible and destructive storm. She was a great devotee of Ibsen and believed that he would set the woman free from her stereotype doll-like existence. She was thankful to Ibsen and expressed her gratitude "To whom we owe this miracle, we cry out our thanks, we can no longer bear this heavy debt of gratitude in silence."[47]

Ibsen's women characters were modelled after all these ardent supporters of feminism of the 1890s and 80s. Ibsen believed in women and especially in the women of his country. All his women characters including Nora, Mrs. Alving or Rebecca West or Hedda Gabler were capable of attracting society in both the ways: first they aroused a sense of an oncoming fear and received severe criticism, disgust and secondly, they were hailed with even warmer enthusiasm by the feminists. Elaborating this sense of inspiration aroused by Ibsen, Camilla Collet, in an article "Women in Literature: Native Authors" published in 1874, stated emphatically:

> ...it is our own dear, native born womanliness, which has outlined itself and now sits waiting for the sorcerer who with his wand will restore health and strength, and this sorcerer, this liberator, is none other than Ibsen himself.[48]

Ibsen always took a positive attitude towards his feminist contemporaries and these women reacted to Ibsen and all the women characters created by him enthusiastically and appreciatively. They acknowledged the contribution made by Ibsen to the creation of a new race of women. As Shaw was an ardent disciple of Ibsen he carried this "new race" of independent, self-complacent women carving a niche by expressing the importance of individual will. Shaw never projected womanly ideal created since Shakespearean times. The long accepted concept of "Womanly woman," Woman as a "paragon" and an "ideal," as depicted in Victorian literature, found no ambience in Shaw's plays. If we observe the traditional Victorian woman's concept infused in society, it will help us in determining women's place in literature keeping in view Arnold's concept that "literature is the mirror of society."

In the Victorian society the principal career open to women was only marriage and home, business life was not for them. Observing this fact Ivor Brown has observed, "women's place...continued to be home...business life has not to be invaded by feminine trespassers."[49] The Victorian girls were taught to repress and conceal her thoughts, feelings, desires and to observe self censorship which was a kind of inhibition. Catching the trauma imposed upon women, Jan Vaughan Pinckney comments:

> Women are greater dissemblers than men.... By habit, moral training and modern education, they are obliged to do so. The very first lessons of infancy teach them to repress their feelings, control their very thoughts.[50]

The glorification of the wifely and maternal role flourished in the eighteenth and nineteenth centuries as "the feminine ideal" which was later named as "feminine mystique" by Betty Frieden.[51] This ideal necessitated that women by nature were required to be submissive and domesticated. It was a divine gift determined by the biological factors and requirements. Women who were frustrated and unsatisfied with the limits set for them were treated as subversive or neurotic. Explaining the Victorian ideals concerned with women Nancy F. Cott writes:

> The middle class ideology of the proper sphere of womanhood, which developed in post-industrial England and America, prescribed a woman who would be a perfect lady, an Angel in the House, contentedly submissive to men, but strong in her inner purity and religiosity, queen in her own realm of the Home.[52]

By the time Shaw came to the theatre there was much progress in the condition of the female. She could join the theatre and take up the job of teacher, nurse or governess—all considered to be an extension of feminine virtues. It was not considered to be unwomanly to live by the pen. Shaw's mother Lucinda Elizabeth Gurley had an instinctive love for music and she had to make it the chief profession under circumstantial necessity. Shaw's elder sister, Lucy joined Carl Roza Opera Company and rose as high as to get the leading role in the very popular piece called *Dorothy*. Fiction was soon to provide some profitable careers for women novelists to express their pent up feelings and their rebellious but silent protest against male dominated society. Upon the use of Fiction as a means of expression, Showalter writes:

> Few English women writers openly advocated the use of Fiction as revenge against a patriarchal society (as did the American novelist Fanny Fern, for example), but many confessed to sentiments of "maternal feelings sisterly affection, esprit de corps" for their readers.[53]

The Brontës were the pioneers who came out of patronage; Mary Ann Evans wrote under the pseudonym of George Eliot and proved herself to be a novelist of high reputation with a large readership. Novel translated the felt pain and oppression of women into the championship of mill workers, child labourers, prostitutes and slaves. From Jane Austen to George Eliot, the women's novel moved, in spite of restrictions and curbs, in the direction of an "all inclusive female realism." It became a wide, socially informed investigating discovery of the daily lives and values of women within the family and the community which marked a declaration of independence, in the female tradition. Apart from writing profession women came forward to work in factories and industries. Experiencing this change Ivor Brown writes:

> Now there is so much work to be done in commerce and industry, such insistence on continual increase of output, and so vigorous a demand for the labour of both sexes that we may be surprised to find Victorian society economically viable while myriads of hands were deflected to domestic service. Any family with social ranking of the humblest kind had to keep a resident maid in order not to be disgraced.[54]

The value of feminine labour increased with the upturn in demands for all kinds of feminine labour including some highly paid positions. Girls were being paid reasonably well for a business job too. The feminine typists at last swarmed into the cities. This aggravated the chances of mating; so the middle class girl did not have to wait at home for a husband. The necessary step in the liberation of women was the right to work, to be admitted to the professions where they could prove their competence. Married Women's Property Act in 1882, made it possible that property of wives would be legally their own. This act reduced, if not wholly abolished, a gross inequality. The War of 1914-18 proved to be a liberator of women who came out of their houses and demanded the right to vote in national and local elections which was ultimately given to them in the Act of 1918 and amended in 1928 giving right to vote on the same scale as the masculine enfranchisement. The drastic change, seen in the condition of working women, made Ivor Brown observe:

> The mistress of a quite prosperous home is now the stay-at-home drudge. Her daughters go out to earn wages or salaries and make their spare time a good time. Shaw's indignation at the neglect of young woman's capacities and the humiliations of the marriage market is now completely out-of-date, today if they have energy and ability they can go almost anywhere and practise almost any profession.[55]

Shaw had already predicted this social metamorphosis to his boyhood friend Mathew Edward Mc Nutt:

> The Victorian theory about women is ludicrous delusion. She is the most dangerous of all the animals, if you come to that view of the situation. The attempt to hypnotize her into believing herself weak was bound to fail; and it has.[56]

Woman was retrieving her position in the society, and this was reflected in literature. Shaw admitted in *Mrs. Warren's Profession* in 1898 that "a new woman was already arriving, one who was determined to make a decent living without angling for a husband or otherwise selling her charms. She could now do so because at last a few professional opportunities were becoming open to women."[57] Observing the somewhat miserable and pitiable condition portrayed in contemporary drama, Shaw commented that "Men in their writing were perpetually making the feminine creature more feminine than she wants to be."[58] This shows the relationship between male writers and the female characters created by them, who often showed lack of personal sympathy. They projected her as a meek, mild creature unable to establish herself as an individual without a man. Commenting on this lacuna of literature Barbara Watson has critically observed: "The inability to create women characters is only one sign of something wrong in the literary treatment of women."[59] The chief reason behind this apathy towards women was that they were viewed as sexual objects; a commodity either to be used or extolled as paragon who had no desire for herself. Probing the significance of this feminine projection Watson writes, "In writing about woman, that imagination has had to be artificially fired either by sexual interest or by the doubly artificial device, that has produced paragons...."[60]

By and by a change in the literary perception of women began to take place. Literature started voicing the sensibilities of women. Jane Austen, George Eliot, the Brontë sisters had already given a genuine existence to them in their literary work. Meredith, Henry James showed women's participation in life as integral and inestimable as that of men. Theatre virtually excluded women for a long time because drama was the most traditional and conservative of all the arts, which had a negative perception of women. Writing about the condescending image created by Theatre, Nancy Reinhardt said that the theatre was a public and social institution which was male dominated. The popular image of actresses was that of a scarlet woman and the reason behind this was the puritanic attitude towards entertainment and that was why women were not allowed to display themselves in the theatre.[61] During the nineteenth and twentieth centuries theatre became respectable and was accepted as a profession for both men and women; the opportunities of demanding female parts at turn-of-the century European drama brought fame to Ellen Terry, Elizabeth Robins, Sarah Benhardt, Mrs. Patrick Campbell, Florence Farr and others.

Such developments helped Shaw formulate his views about women in general which had an effect on his women characters. *The Quintessence of Ibsenism* sums up Shaw's image of woman in the chapter titled "The Womanly Woman". He wrote that this feminine document rescued an ungrateful generation from Materialism and Rationalism. The first four chapters of this book broke up homes and made suffragettes in the most unexpected ways. He criticized the ordinary conforming female, the ideal of womanliness and self sacrificing women who were not only taken advantage of but disliked as well for their pains. When men don't feel supreme satisfaction in self sacrifice why should women feel contentment. Shaw repudiated the romantic notion of self surrender as a crucial factor in true womanly love and expressed that its repulsive effect could be felt by both the sexes. He wrote, "Love loses its charm when it is not free...the successful wooer, in both sexes alike, is the one who can stand out for honourable conditions, and, failing them, go without."[62] This shows that Shaw gave equal opportunity to both the sexes for the expression of love and freedom, if anyone would try to be possessive or submissive, the existence of love would subside. Self respectability should be the yardstick to perpetrate it otherwise whether men or women, they would be good-for-nothing. Women are never taken as an "end" in themselves, like men; rather they are a commodity, means of ministering to men's "appetite." A woman becomes an ideal wife when she does everything that the ideal husband likes, and nothing else.

Criticising this prevalent concept of an ideal wife, Shaw wrote that the treatment of women denied them the right to live that was insufferable to any human being. Women deceive themselves by conceptualising that the sublime devotion they show to men as husbands, exalts them and renders them "blest." Men themselves help women maintain this illusion as disillusionment will break the "affectionate tie" and degrade them. Idealist illusions arise from a social notion that: "a vocation for domestic management and the care of children is natural to women, and that women who lack them are not women at all, but members of the third, or Bashkirtseff sex."[63] Shaw directed all the women to repudiate their age-old womanliness and duty to their relatives in order to assert their own freedom and individuality. They were not to consider men as their masters and themselves as slaves. In fact, they were not the slave of any man but slaves of duty which bound them.

Shaw viewed women as equal to men; he did not regard them as animals of another species. In his viewpoint "sexes wear different boots and bonnets not different souls."[64] As a propounder of radical feminist views Shaw came to the conclusion that the nature of a human being was neither masculine nor feminine exclusively, but a mixture of the two. The attributes of womanliness and manliness owe more to the environmental and conventional pressures; these are not natural, deep-rooted traits of personality. His concept of sexual equality is an expression of his androgynous ideology, which has under currents of Virginia Woolf's thoughts and some other modern feminists writers. Simone de Beauvoir has expressed that the semi-slavery of woman is due to the social and educational situation of society, where she has been tutored to be shy, passive and deprived of her usual responsibilities as a natural human being.[65] The notion of "passivity" develops in her from childhood and is not a biological datum; it is in fact an imposed destiny upon her by her oppressors and the makers of society. A woman who has received boyish upbringing, very largely escapes the defects of feminity, and it is only the father who can give such type of education. But in case of bringing up a child, he has a secondary role. A mother respects the maleness of her son and leads her daughter into the weak and passive feminity.[66] In the view of Julia Kristeva "It is not the biological sex of a person, but the subject position she or he takes up, that determines their revolutionary potential."[67]

Kristeva favours women's objection to the dichotomy between masculine and feminine as metaphysical. Her theory of bisexuality echoes the feminist stand of Virginia Woolf (some sixty years earlier), the founding mother of contemporary debate, who foreshadowed the future development so acutely that feminists from various critical positions—Marxist, psychoanalytical, post-structuralist—look at her for inspiration and support. In Woolf's view, Androgyny is a "full balance and command of an emotional range that includes male and female elements."[68] Showalter clarifies that Woolf's concept of androgyny is not a flight from fixed gender identities but a recognition of their falsifying metaphysical nature. Woolf does not flee away from such gender identities due to fear; rather she discards them for what they are. She conveys that the goal of feminist struggle must be to "deconstruct the death dealing binary oppositions of masculinity and feminity."[69] Bernard Shaw also demanded the rejection of gender roles while supporting a "theory that demands the deconstruction of sexual identity [which] is indeed authentically feminist."[70] Some feminist critics raise the question that whether men can be feminists or not as only women can be feminists by virtue of being women. Explaining the relation between man and feminism, Stephen Heath writes that this relation:

> ...involves learning new ways of being women and men against and as an end to the reality of women's oppression...women are the subjects of feminism, its initiators, its makers, its force; the move and the join from being a woman to being a feminist is the grasp of that subjecthood. Men are the objects, part of analysis, agents of the structure to be transformed, representative in, carriers of the patriarchal mode...[71]

Definitely the patriarchal structure has to be changed but by rejecting the entity of men it cannot be changed. It can be transformed when men are part of feminist ideology and movement so that their patriarchal, male characteristic outlook of superiority may be modified to grant the equal status to women. Women become feminists because the relation between the lived experience and feminism is better understood by them. It is somewhat a first hand experience for them and a second hand experience for men. But men can be feminists if we take it from androgynous point of view. Woolf insisted that the mind of the artist should be androgynous. She wrote:

> If one is a man, still the woman part of brain must have effect; and a woman also must have intercourse with the man in her. Coleridge perhaps meant this when he said that a great mind is androgynous. It is when this fusion takes place that the mind is fully fertilized and uses all its faculties. Perhaps a mind that is purely masculine cannot create any more than a mind that is purely feminine.[72]

Clinical psychology has also advocated that a creative writer or an individual whether male or female encompasses "masculine" and "feminine" qualities. Bernard Shaw always assumed that a woman was a person exactly like himself. It does not mean that Shaw advocated the denial of feminity but it was as Watson points out "...by no means a plea for the masculine woman. What he meant was not to repudiate feminity but to assert its social values; not to ape masculinity but to demonstrate its insufficiency."[73]

The first step Shaw took for the emancipation was the creation of such a woman who stripped away the invisible bonds of patriarchal system which captivated the women of the Victorian Age and literature. While opening the social shackles of woman in his plays, he invented a vibrant, self-willed, sprightly woman having all the virtues which were associated with males so far. His women characters indulge in a kind of rebellion against the lady like standards set down for their behaviour in the 1880s. Emancipation of these women led to a kind of improvisation of manners, faced by both women and Negroes in the twentieth century. Women in Shaw, possess two unwomanly virtues—wit and will; these have been admired and appreciated by Shaw just against the prudent literary tradition of deprecating such type of women. They have been endowed with a verbal grace and arrogance which is the sign or symbol of newly won freedom.

Mrs. George in *Getting Married* says that the women are all different but it is the men who are all alike. It seems that Shaw has put his own ideas about women through these words. Undoubtedly Shaw has created a galaxy of women characters and each character with different set of characteristics and mannerisms. Elaborating on the kaleidoscope of Shaw's characters Purdom has observed:

> Each of [these]...characters deserves praise. For Shaw could create admirable secondary characters, as can all good dramatists but genius resides in the leading characters. Shaw lives by .virtue of Bluntschli, Marchbanks.... Major Barbara and Saint Joan as Shakespeare lives by...Rosalind, Viola....[74]

Shaw never put on the stage women with their womanly weaknesses in the throes of patriarchal notion; instead he envisaged real men and women with genuine follies and intellect. Considering this real life portrayal of dramatis personae, Purdom states:

> He was not concerned to put upon the stage men and women in their lives of weakness, confusion and commonness, or natural life in its monotony, but living people in their hidden selves, displayed in their bright hues of their masked absurdities.[75]

Shaw openly asserted his viewpoint about woman that she was an individual and not a lifeless object nor a sexual impetus. He gave his women characters their own individualities and choices as human beings. In proclaiming their own rights to existence his women characters are sometimes accused of being eccentric and egotist; but this unconventionality gives them an everlasting charm and triumph that marks a genuine importance as protagonists.

The titles of Shaw's major plays indicate the essential and great importance of women in his work: *Candida, Mrs. Warren's Profession, Major Barbara, St. Joan. The Millionairess*—these titles suggest the women protagonist in respect to social ambience around them. One very important fact about the male characters in Shavian drama is that, generally all of them are supportive of the Shavian women. It seems that women have a superior goal and that men are their assistants in the accomplishment of their objectives. This observation has been highlighted by Watson who says that "the only men who are a match for the Shavian women are those who have given up the old illusions about the relations between the sexes".[76] It means a new men community which can accept the equality of women, has been evolved in Shaw's plays.

Shaw accepted the metaphysical principle that "Will" is the essence of real existence, propounded by the great German philosopher Schopenhauer who viewed this "Will" striving endlessly, purposelessly and blindly. Shaw named this "Will" as "Life Force": a supreme power beyond the principle of sufficient reason with a profound purpose of Evolution. This supreme power manifests itself in all individuals and is utilised by them for fulfilling different purposes in which each of them is involved. For example, in *Saint Joan* Life Force takes the form of celibacy and sainthood. Such a "Will" may be in opposition to the conventions, to reasonable compromise, but in the vital person it is never in opposition to the individual will. For this purpose it guides human beings' activities, actions with an evolutionary vision of creating a better future generation. This "Will" or "Life-Force" is unconsciously active, creative but not blind as Schopenhauer advocated. The "Life-Force" continually strives to improve on its own creations, just as an artist endeavours for more perfect manifestation of his creation. According to the view point of Shaw it is the energy, forcefulness of "Life-Force" that directs mother-woman to hunt for a suitable father for the procreation of a superhuman: a better progeny than forefathers and in accomplishing this task of nature, man is only an assistant of woman—who is creator fulfilling the evolutionary purpose of "Life-Force."

Shaw's concept of equal status for men and women never demanded masculinisation of women through dresses. He never wanted women to be dressed in masculine costumes as it caused them to lose their feminity, womanly charms and thus look ridiculous. It does not mean that he recommended Victorian voluminous gowns either, which covered a woman from head-to-toe. He criticised Victorian costumes as these concealed the fact that women were human beings. Shaw's description of Mrs. Clandon, one of the new and advanced women, in *You Never Can Tell* presents her as he wanted a woman to be:

> She has never made herself ugly or ridiculous by affecting masculine waistcoats, collars and watch chains, like some of her old comrades who had more aggressiveness than taste.... She therefore dresses in as businesslike a way as she can without making a guy of herself, ruling out all attempts at sex attraction and imposing respect on frivolous mankind and fashionable womankind.[77]

This is suggestive of the fact that women can get respect and adoration without dressing themselves in manly ways. Shaw upheld the notion that women were women and they should not try to imitate men. Germain Greer, in the twenty-first century, has advocated a new feminist theory which rejects the imitation of men and their manly patterns of behaviour in order to acquire equality. Of late, feminists argue that a woman has a different personality and different traits. She should be treated as a woman with her own original thoughts and desires and not behave like a man. Shaw had expressed similar views just a century back.

Shaw revolted against the sentimental heroine—an ideal which made her a paragon and priestess and ultimately a prisoner. By a paragon he meant placing a woman on a pedestal by man and making her a prisoner who was tied with virtual fetters. Man was, on one side, her protector and on the other her slave—a slave of her charms. Shaw's first literary work *My Dear Dorothea* was related to a little girl. The inherent theme of this work was the spiritual management of woman's life in an unmanaged and mismanaged society. He expressed in it that women had to observe submissiveness to authority whether to God, of nature or to the fundamental social order of dichotomy which rendered a woman a lopsided place; this deprivation of woman as a human being became a point of intellectual attack in Shaw's plays.

The qualities Shaw tried to inculcate in his multidimensional women were of spiritual concerns i.e.

> Qualities of spirit; discontent, proper hypocrisy, pride, individuality, self control, politeness.... They prepare her to be a certain kind of human being and to save her soul inside her irrelevant petticoats and corsets.[78]

He taught the lesson of selfishness, i.e. in Shavian sense an expression of self not suppression of it. This was the central message of Shaw to women. Watson thinks that this is the main element of Shaw's advice and the concept of "Shavian selfishness" which is so radically shocking now as it was then. He prohibited women from taking the advice of others as it could develop into a life long habit of transforming them into parasites without the power of independent mental attitude. The persona that characterizes a Shavian heroine is of unconventional, intelligent woman with a will of her own. She knows the befooling illusions of society and therefore is an aggressive rebel against the stereotype paragon sentimental image of woman. It is because Shaw took women not as schmaltzy, culture-obsessed sex symbols but as fellow beings giving a vent for id, ego, and libido. He insisted that women were not angels but ordinary fallible creatures, subject to temper tantrums, sexual infatuation and other lapses from decorum. In this way Shaw prepared men to visualize women as human beings who had to be granted equal importance.

Many good critics are averse to Bernard Shaw's non-conformist, unladylike New Woman. They accuse Shaw of diverting women from commonly accepted female culture concept. Frank Harris calls his women "sexless dolls".[79] They have been defined by critics as "men in petticoats," "unsentimental," "unromantic," "rebellion," "cruel" etc. Recent studies show that Shaw has "masculinised" his female species. Talking about the most uncommon women in the Shavian canon, Leon Hugo has commented "One should not sentimentalise over a girl whose hard headedness and brisk decisiveness finally rout all sentimentality and all 'beauty and romance' and encourages her to take 'life as it is'".[80]

Of course he condemns thick-skinned Vivie who epitomizes brainy and strong-headed women successful and efficient outside the custom of marriage and motherhood. Another much despised woman is Blanche portrayed without artistic credibility. Commenting on her Hugo thinks that, "one senses in Blanche the hesitant, barely articulated beginning of that driving force which was to bring so many Shaw's women to compelling utterance".[81] Blanche heralds the arrival of the army of aggressive women. She marks the genesis of unsentimental, invulnerable, driven by life-force kind of woman. Critics probing the complexities of new women have observed that, in creating this shade of woman, Shaw goes a step further from the conventional "new woman" and creates a woman who arouses our sympathy in spite of being independent and emancipated. As Hugo writes, "he has created a woman whose emancipation affords room for pity".[82] Women in Shaw get freedom of individuality by putting their feminine charm and humanity at stake.

Another despicable trait of Shaw's women in the eye of critics is that they are "the idealisation of the freedom fighters." On this point, Sagittarius asks, "was his paragon the idealisation of freedom fighters who to the everlasting credit of their sex had banged the front door, and borne the banner 'Votes for Women' through the streets...?".[83] He criticizes Shaw's working women as "shocking toadies or incorrigible rascals." Commenting on the manly attitude of New Woman, a critic writes "the New Woman of Shaw's conception is thus a degenerate hybrid with women's body and man's mental and emotional toughness and is unfitted for her natural avocation".[84] She has also given evidence of Shaw's dried relationship with his mother, sister and other women. His knowledge of woman is second hand; whatever he has observed are only the characteristics depicting company manners and conventional behaviour.

Some critics view Shavian Women as cold-blooded virile, sexless and some, on the other hand, judge them as sex initiators. In some plays women are the dominant partners in man-woman relationship taking initiative to express their passion of love. According to Ivor Brown "So much is man made to seem a victim of the instrument employed by the female in her instinctive compliance with the Life Force, its demand for fertility, and its self continuing process."[85] [Brown and Frank Harris harbour just opposite viewpoints.] Despite all these violations of set standards of female code of conduct Shaw's women are winners and victors. This is also one of the allegations against them. They act according to their conscience and are not dependent on destiny and society.

Despite all these allegations and counter allegations Shaw had a discerning insight into women's soul which revealed a potential of inherent power and strength in them who, without recognising its value, struggled against society. How did he get this clue of the inner strength of women? If we examine Shaw's life, it is apparent that his whole personality was an offshoot of his multifaceted relationship with a number of women—right from his own mother, Lucinda to his wife Charlotte. According to Michael Holroyd there were three categories of women in his life who had three different types of influences upon him—"flirtations with single women, usually at this time young Fabian girls; philanderings with the wives of friends, usually socialist colleagues; and a consummated love affair with a divorced or separated lady."[86]

Shaw's relationship with women in his life is reflected in the creation of strong women characters. Most of the female characters inherited prominent traits of those women who had a liaison with Shaw. Emphasizing the influence of real-life-women on the work and life of Shaw C.G. Du Cann has observed:

> It is high time that more credit was given to such figures in Shaw's womanizing as Florence Farr, Annie Besant and Mrs. Patrick Campbell than either Shaw or his biographers-to-date have been willing to concede.[87]

If an astute observation is made on Shaw's life-span since childhood up to his old age as nonagenarian, it can help us determine the correlation between reality and art culminating into exploration of deep impression of real life women in Shaw's life on the women characters in his plays. Explaining the relation between art and life, Susanne K. Langer has observed that "the main business of all poetic art is to create an 'illusion of life', which shifts the attention from actuality to fiction. People listen with rapt attention to stories just as they keenly look at pictures."[88] In this definition the words "life" and "illusion" have fixed connotations. "Life" according to Langer, has double interpretations—the first is in the "biological sense,...antithetical to the word death"; second is "social application...what happens or what the living being encounters and copes with."[89] This second implication creates the realm of poetic art. By "illusion" she means the image of the experienced events of life projected in a work of art with various modes, tricks. In this way a work of art is partly a poetic creation and partly an experience which gets value by its ability to communicate as it is not pleasurable in silence and privacy. Experience gives it a "sense of life" and this "livingness" establishes a close relationship between art and life. As David Daiches has written that "events observed in real life are not literary elements but materials for literature."[90] A writer transforms this by his imagination. For a true writer his own life is a theme which gets the colours with the use of language. This observation sets a relationship between literature and life which is true in the case of Bernard Shaw. The dramatist had different types of relationships with women of substance not with common, ordinary women. He loved falling in love with women and thus exploring the individuals to discover and continue burning the flame of his passion for writing. He wrote:

> I am fond of women (or one in a thousand, say), but I am in earnest about quite other things. To most women one man and one life time make a world. I require the whole populations and historical epochs to engage my

> interests seriously and make the writing machine (for that is what G.B.S. is) work at full speed and pressure. Love is only diversion and recreation to me.[91]

Beatrice Webb also figured out that Shaw philandered with remarkable women just to acquire material for his writings. He was never in earnest on any of the involvements. He was an explorer of relationships, "a sprite" in love affairs, not a "real person" and nobody can have a static romance with a "sprite."[92]

Lucinda Elizabeth Gurly, Shaw's mother was the model Shavian woman in many respects both emotionally and economically. Shaw wrote in *Cashel Byron's Profession*, "I have a mother; I have not seen her for years; and I don't much care if I never see her. It was through her that I came to be what I am."[93] This statement summarises the importance of Shaw's mother in the formation of the ideal woman; his own personal life being devoid of motherly care. He was no mother's boy although an only son. When the Shaws arrived in London in 1876, they relied on their mother for the essential, vital things of life. He did not partake in the struggling life as his mother did, who shouldered the family burden by earning livelihood and managing household chores. He was very much influenced by his mother and projected her in a very different way. He wrote: "Technically speaking I should say she was the worst mother conceivable...however...incapable of unkindness to any child, animal, or flower, or indeed to any person or thing whatsoever."[94] He wrote that his mother had self-sufficiency and power of solitude to an extent which kept her up under circumstances that certainly would have crushed or baffled any other woman. On the one hand, he deprecated his mother's lack of motherly touch and sensibilities and on the other, he appreciated the self-complacency of his mother who fought against circumstantial compulsion. All these supported Shaw to idolize her to the utmost pitch of imagination without illusions. It is because of this fact that he delineated woman as a procreator yet not a conventional mother. It might be that he drew the image of superwomen from his mother and developed perspicacious women who:

> ...conquered all ties of blood, whose arch passion has defeated all passions in her—even the maternal passion insofar as it is a weakness, it was this mother who was 'the worst possible mother' and yet Shaw would not have changed for the best mother in the world.[95]

This is the reason that in Shavian plays parents-children relationship is devoid of sentimentality, particularly in *Mrs. Warren's Profession* and some other plays.

In his relationship with other women Shaw was very much balanced. Undoubtedly he had many affairs but all were of different kinds not worldly or carnal. Hesketh Pearson describing this balance writes:

> The fact that they were not of primary importance in his life is balanced by the fact that he often made them of primary importance in his art, the explanation of which is that they always appealed far more to his imagination than to his bodily needs.[96]

He believed in ideal and platonic relationship with women although he had physical relationship in early manhood. Even his married life with Charlotte was unconsummated in the sense of physical relationship. He thought that imagined love played more important part in life than real love as it ceased to exist after a certain period. He took love in black and white—through letters the supreme form of love as it never lacked its charm.

Shaw had relationships not with the run-of-the-mill, ordinary women but with unconventional women. Alice Locket, Jenny Patterson, Florence Farr, Annie Besant, May Morris, Eleanor Marx-Aveling, Edith Nesbit, Janet Achurch, Ellen Terry, Mrs. Patrick Campbell, Molly Tompkins were few astounding and remarkable women who had ardent associations with Shaw. All these remarkable women had their different influences on Shaw's conception of women. Somewhere Shaw's women characters have the same habits and tendencies as all these women had. Shaw was completely susceptible to feminine beauty and charm, especially when they were conveyed to him through the medium of art.

Shaw commenced his romantic relationship with Ellen Terry not because she was a wonderful woman but because she was an impeccable actress. He thought of May Morris as his "Celestial Bride" with whom a "Mystic Betrothal was registered in Heaven."[97] Annie Besant, the best platform orator of her generation, had very intense and intimate relationship with Shaw for a long time which changed her course of life; but at last her unrequited passion of love for Shaw led her to lead a Shawless life. Mrs. Jenny Patterson, one of his mother's singing pupils, virtually raped him at the age of twenty-nine. This was the first time when he was sexually infatuated. After that Shaw seldom got physically obsessed and enraptured. On the contrary women found him attractive and irresistible and threw their arms round him declaring their adoration for him. Jenny Patterson was a jealous termagant who created scenes later in Shaw's life whenever she discovered Shaw's association with any other woman. She was the model for Julia in *The Philanderer* and Blanche in *Widowers' Houses*. Florence Farr was a young independent professional woman, who enjoyed an exceptional freedom of social interaction in artistic circles in London. As she was good-natured and very good looking all her men friends fell in love with her. She was incapable of jealousy unlike Jenny Patterson. She had her Leporello list which contained fourteen names of those who proposed to her in 1894. Here she resembles Lina Szczepanowska in *Misalliance*. Lina has also one list of her wooers which makes her feel proud of herself. Another woman in Shaw's life was Eleanor Marx Aveling, daughter of Karl Marx. She was one of the Dark Ladies, very striking in appearance and very clever. She was a very daring woman who decided to shack up with Dr. Edward Aveling and consequently burnt her boats. But like Annie Besant she was a social rebel who unfortunately met a deadly end. With Ellen Terry Shaw had "the ideal affair...one conducted by post."[98] Shaw wrote *Captain Brassbound's Conversion*, and its heroine Lady Cicily Waynflete was modelled on Ellen Terry.[99] With Ellen Shaw had the most prolonged and most literary romance. Mrs. Patrick Campbell had beauty as well as brains who took London by storm in one night as Pinero's *The Second Mrs. Tanqueray*. She alone—of all Shaw's women—could have broken his marriage with Charlotte. She was the "best-hated and most feared woman in her profession at the height of her fame."[100] At rehearsals on Shaw's play *Pygmalion*, she flung a pair of slippers into the face of Sir Herbert Beerbohm Tree with such force that he collapsed in tears. As an actress she dared to utter the-then-shocking words in public, "Not bloody likely" with the same native force of reality as Stella [Mrs. Patrick].[101] Shaw fell in love with Mrs. Patrick and felt like marrying her but she got married to her second husband George Cornwallis-West. Janet Achurch was one of the beautiful actresses who captured Shaw's attention; he wrote *Candida* for her and modelled the character of the heroine after her.[102]

Shaw got married to Charlotte Payne-Townshed, younger daughter of an Irish barrister and landowner. As a small child she had declared that she would marry a "genius" and was called "one of the 'New Women' of her day, with ideas of having a life of her own and developing herself."[103] Bernard Shaw and Charlotte were certainly no Romeo and Juliet. Shaw wrote to Frank Harris in 1930 that "As man and wife, we found a new relation in which sex had no part. It ended the old gallantries, flirtations and philanderings for both of us."[104] She was the driving force behind his greatest creation, *Saint Joan*, the symbol of a heroic woman.

Thus Shaw's characters display a beautiful amalgam of fact with fiction to create dramatic illusion; these creations were not only valid in his age but proved to be forceful and cogent in the future also; and today, a century later, we can still approve of the Shavian women, who do not appear to be outdated or behind the times.

REFERENCES

1. Michael R. Booth, *Preface to English Nineteenth Century Theatre* (Manchester: Manchester University Press, 1988), pp. 1-2.
2. *Ibid*, p. x.
3. *Ibid*, p. xi.
4. Raymond Williams, *Drama—From Ibsen to Brecht* (London: Chatto and Windus, 1971), p. 27.
5. Michael R. Booth, *Preface to English Nineteenth Century Theatre*, p. 3.
6. Hugh Hunt, Kenneth Richards, John Russell Taylor, *The Revels History of Drama in English*, Vol. VII, 1880 to the Present Day, (London: Meshuen and Co. Ltd., 1978), p. 1.

7. Michael R. Booth, *Preface to English Nineteenth Century Theatre*, pp. 35-36.
8. Patricia D. Denison, "Victorian and Modern Drama: Social Convention and Theatrical Invention in T.W. Robertson's Plays" *Modern Drama*, 37 (1994), pp. 403-404.
9. *Ibid*, p. 413.
10. *Ibid*.
11. John Gassner and Quinn Edward (ed.), *The Reader's Encyclopaedia of World Drama* (London: Methuen and Co. Ltd. 1970), pp. 234-235.
12. Hugh Hunt, Kenneth Richards, John Russell Taylor, *The Revels History of Drama in English*, p. 166.
13. John Gassner and Quinn Edward (ed.), *The Reader's Encyclopaedia of World Drama*, p. 236.
14. Raymond Williams, Drama—*From Ibsen to Brecht*, p. 25.
15. *Ibid*.
16. George Bernard Shaw, *The Quintessence of Ibsenism* (London: Constable & Co., 1913), p. xix.
17. *Ibid*, p. viii.
18. *Ibid*, p. x.
19. Raymond Williams, Drama—*From Ibsen to Brecht*, p. 32.
20. *Ibid*, p. 39.
21. Robert W. Corrigan, *The Modern Theatre*, (New York: The Macmillan Company, 1966), pp. ix-x.
22. Christopher Innes, *Modern British Drama 1890-1990*, (Cambridge: Cambridge University Press, 1992), p. 2.
23. Margery M. Morgan, *The Shavian Playground: An exploration of the Art of George Benard Shaw* (London: Methuen and Co. Ltd., 1972), p. 5.
24. *Ibid*, pp. 5-6.
25. *Ibid*, p. 237.
26. *Ibid*.
27. Eric Bently, "The Making of a Dramatist (1892-1903)" *G.B. Shaw: A Collection of Critical Essays*, ed. R.J. Kaufmann, (New Jersey: Prentice-Hall, Inc., 1965), p. 58.
28. *Ibid*, p. 66.
29. John Gassner and Quinn Edward (ed.), *The Reader's Encyclopaedia of World Drama*, pp. 238-239.

30. Elaine Showalter, *A Literature of Their Own: British Women Novelists from Bronte to Lessing* (New Jersey: Princeton University Press, 1977), p. 182.
31. Elaine Showalter (ed.), *Women's Liberation and Literature*, (New York: Harcourt Brace Jovanovich, Inc. 1971), p. 9.
32. Gail Finney, *Women in Modern Drama: Freud, Feminism and European Theatre at the Turn of the Century* (London: Corvell University Press, 1989), p. 6.
33. *Ibid*, p. 5.
34. Elaine Showalter (ed.), *Women's Liberntion and Literature*, p. 13.
35. Gail Finney, *Women in Modern Drama: Freud, Feminism and European Theatre at the Turn of the Century*, p. 4.
36. Elaine Showalter (ed.), *Women's Liberation and Literature*, p. 1.
37. Gail Finney, *Women in Modern Drama: Freud, Feminism and European Theatre at the Turn of the Century*, p. 13.
38. Gareth Griffith, *Socialism And Superior Brains: The Political Thought of Bernard Shaw*, (London: Routledge, 1993), p. 157.
39. Gail Finney, *Women in Modern Drama: Freud, Feminism and European Theatre at the Turn of the Century*, p. 195.
40. Carolyn Forrey, "The New Woman Revisited," *Women's Studies*, 2 (1974), p. 38.
41. Kate Trimble Stein, "The Art of Selection," Club Women, December 1897, p. 76.
42. Katherine Hanson, "Ibsen's Women Characters and Their Feminist Contemporaries," *Feminist Theory and Modern Drama: An Anthology of Recent Criticism* ed. Taisha Abraham, (Delhi: Pencraft International, 1998), p. 71.
43. *Ibid.*
44. *Ibid*, p. 72.
45. *Ibid.*
46. *Ibid*, p. 76.
47. *Ibid*, p. 77.
48. *Ibid*, p. 75.
49. Ivor Brown, *Shaw In His Time*, (Edinburgh: Thomas Nelson Ltd., 1965), pp. 91-92.
50. Elaine Showalter, *A Literature of Their Own: British Women Novelists from Bronte to Lessing*, p. 25.
51. Mary Eagleton, *Feminist Literary Criticism*, (London: Longman, 1991), p. 20.

52. Nancy Cott, *Introduction to Roots of Bitterness*, (New York, 1972),
53. Elaine Showalter, *A Literature of Their Own: British Women Novelists from Bronte to Lessing*, p. 16.
54. Ivor Brown, *Shaw In His Time*, p. 91.
55. *Ibid.*
56. Gareth Griffith, *Socialism And Superior Brains: The Political Thought of Bernard Shaw*, p. 159.
57. Ivor Brown, *Shaw In His Time*, p. 98.
58. Barbara Bellow Watson, *A Shavian Guide to the Intelligent Woman* (London: Chatto & Windus, 1964), p. 14.
59. *Ibid.*
60. *Ibid*, p. 16.
61. Julie Holledge, *Innocent Flowers: Women in the Edwardian Theatre* (London: Virago, 1981), p. 7.
62. George Bernard Shaw, *The Quintessence of Ibsenism*, pp. 32-33.
63. *Ibid*, p. 39.
64. Gareth Griffith, *Socialism And Superior Brains: The Political Thought of Bernard Shaw*, p. 161.
65. Simone De Beauvoir, *The Second Sex*, ed. and trans. H.M. Parshley, (London: Vintage, 1997), pp. 269-270.
66. *Ibid*, p. 308.
67. Mary Eagleton, *Feminist Literary Criticism*, p. 46.
68. *Ibid*, p. 29.
69. *Ibid*, pp. 44-46.
70. *Ibid*, pp. 47-48.
71. *Ibid*, p. 194.
72. *Ibid*, p. 170.
73. Barbara Bellow Watson, *A Shavian Guide to the Intelligent Woman*, p. 23.
74. C.B. Purdom, *A Guide to the Plays of Bernard Shaw*, (London: University Paperbacks Methuen, 1963), p. 121.
75. *Ibid*, p. 120.
76. Barbara Bellow Watson, *A Shavian Guide to the Intelligent Woman*, p. 17.
77. George Bernard Shaw, *You Never Can Tell, Bernard Shaw: Complete Plays with Prefaces*, Vol. I to VI (New York: Dodd, Mead and Company, 1962), p. 624.

78. Barbara Bellow Watson, *A Shavian Guide to the Intelligent Woman*, p. 43.

79. Frank Harris, Bernard Shaw: *An Unauthorised Biography based on First-hand Information with a postscript By Mr. Shaw* (New York: Simon and Schurter, 1931), p. 189.

80. Leon Hugo, *Bernard Shaw: Playwrite and Preacher* (London: Methuen and Co. Ltd., 1971), p. 87.

81. *Ibid*, p. 86.

82. *Ibid*, p. 81.

83. Sagittarius, "An Intelligent Woman Guiding the Shavians", *The Shavian*, Vol. 4, Summer 1973: 245-249.

84. Savitri Khanna, "Shaw's Image of Women", *The Shavian*, Vol. 4, Summer 1973: 253-257.

85. Ivor Brown, *Shaw In His Time*, p. 72.

86. Michael Holroyd, *Benard Shaw: The Search for Love*, Vol. 1856-1898, (London: Chatto and Winding, 1988), p. 151.

87. C.G.L. Du Cann, *The Loves of George Bernard Shaw*, (London: Arthur Barker Limited, 1963), p. 15.

88. Susanne K. Langer, *Feeling and Form: A Theory of Art Developed from Philosophy in a New Key* (London: Routledge and Kegan Paul Limited, 1967), p. 213.

89. Meena Sodhi, *Indian English Writing: The Autobiographical Mode*, (New Delhi: Creative Books, 1999), p. 121.

90. *Ibid*, p. 122.

91. C.G.L. Du Cann, *The Loves of George Bernard Shaw*, p. 165.

92. *Ibid*, p. 164.

93. *Ibid*, p. 65.

94. *Ibid*, p. 26.

95. Vinod Bala Sharma, *George Bernard Shaw*, (New Delhi: Prestige Books, 1990), p. 17.

96. Hesketh Pearson, *Bernard Shaw: His Life and Personality* (London: Methuen and Co. Ltd., 1961), p. 109.

97. C.G.L. Du Cann, *The Loves of George Bernard Shaw*, p. 124.

98. *Ibid*, p. 240.

99. *Ibid*, p. 249.

100. *Ibid*, p. 254.

101. *Ibid*, p. 255.

102. *Ibid*, p. 207.

103. *Ibid*, p. 172.

104. *Ibid*, p. 184.

2

Women and Love

As a propounder of the ideology of equality of men and women, Bernard Shaw has given this sense of equality not only in work and politics but in social relationship also. Since centuries women have been looked upon as "object" and men have been the "subject" selecting women for marriage and love without any conscious approach of knowing women's wish and will. They have no right to select and express their feelings of love. But Shaw has turned the table by giving his women characters an open platform to put forward their own choice of their mates. Unlike other Victorian female characters, they never meet bad ends; Shavian society and Shavian characters never criticize the individualities of Shavian women. They openly chase their heartthrobs and entice them with their cunning, unscrupulous tricks without being ashamed in any way; this is because they never believe in false shame. Elaborating this point Barbara Watson writes, "She [The Shavian Woman] does not let her real preference be overruled by false shame."[1] The Shavian woman makes her own assessment and choice without any illusion. When confronted with alternatives she is expected to choose fearlessly on the side of life.[2] All those Shavian women who rise in love [not fall in love because they learn true love] have different shades which in turn have different consequences. Some are childish and impudent who learn lessons. Julia in *The Philanderer* is an immature siren who learns lessons of love. Ann is a representative of those women who are huntress, hunting for the superior men. She is "Everywoman" because she does what woman would naturally do.[3] It seems love is the axis around which all these women revolve articulating the desire for passionate love. Raina has a dream-like element in her; she believes in higher love beyond any real existence. Her disillusionment shatters all the illusions of love and makes her realize what is real love. According to Maurice Valency:

> Raina passes from the one to the other, and in the process is redefined into something more closely approximating her true self. The action thus describes an educational experience which foreshadows the education of Cleopatra, Eliza Doolittle and Barbara Undershaft [not in the sense of love but realism].[4]

Eliza Doolittle in *Pygmalion* and Hypatia in *Misalliance* are also in this category personifying nuances of love. Eliza, a flower girl turns into a glorious maiden learning to love a human being not a superman. Hypatia is in love with the concept of love, she wants love because she wants something to happen. Through these women, Shaw has explored the realm of women's heart providing her with the equal opportunity to verbalize her choice. Whether they win or lose this is not the matter of concern, the concern is that they broke the ice. In fact, all these women are the agents of life force and are in search of better fathers for their future children.

Man and Superman is a play wherein comedy is dovetailed with philosophy very adroitly. Comedy of sexual relationship between man and woman has been merged with an exposition of the idea of Life Force. Life Force, Shaw feels, makes man and woman comical, sexual puppets for its higher and superior purpose wherein a woman is assigned the role of a huntress in search of her suitable competent prey to fulfil the nature's purpose of evolving a superman. Shaw's extreme faith in "Eugenics" is the underlying theme of *Man and Superman*. Through Ann Shaw has propounded an explosive concept of woman initiating physical relationship. Commenting on this startling idea of Shaw, Purdom writes:

> The relations between the sexes are displayed as the 'love chase of the man by the woman'...'man is not victor in the duel of sex' is the idea around which the simple comedy is built: an idea of natural biology. Man is

> helpless in a woman's hands; says Shaw, and in 1903, when the play was published people found it shocking, for it wasn't nice to say that the initiative in sex was with the woman.[5]

Shaw's concept of women is that they are men's driving force, that which gives birth, which makes men overcome their natural inertia and become creators as women naturally are. Shaw has projected Ann as an incarnation of this idea of the driving force.

Ann Whitefield has two potential marriage partners and the plot development exposes the rejection of one and capitulation to marriage of the other. These two partners are Octavius Robinson and John Tanner respectively. Octavius is madly in love with Ann or in other words Octavius's "whole soul is absorbed by Ann." (Act I) Ann is clever enough to grind her own axe. Despite Tanner's direct allusions to Ann's unscrupulousness, Octavius keeps on extolling her charm and beauty or it can be assumed that Ann leaves such an indelible impression on him that ensnares him to her throughout the play: she never disillusions him. Shaw verbalises this illusion:

> To Octavius she is an enchantingly beautiful woman, in whose presence the world becomes transfigured.... She is to him the reality of romance, the inner good sense of nonsense, the unveiling of his eyes, the freeing of his soul, the abolition of time place, and circumstance, the etherealization of his blood into rapturous rivers of the very water of life itself, the revelation of all the mysteries and the sanctification of all the dogmas.[6] (Act I)

Ann is Octavius's inspiration, yet she rejects him. Ann coaxes him, cajoles him to give up his love-chase; at the same time he should sustain his adulation:

> ANN. Always is a long word, Tavy. You see, I shall have to live up always to your idea of my divinity; and I don't think I could do that if we were married. But if I marry Jack [Tanner] you'll never be disillusioned—at least not until I grow old.[7] (Act IV)

Ann's refusal to Octavius exemplifies the concept that a Shavian woman never believes in romantic ideals. Whenever there is confrontation between real life pursuits and poetic life, Shavian woman takes the side of life. Revealing this attitude Barbara Watson has written:

> The Shavian heroine (or hero) is expected to assess herself and her choices without illusion. And between her alternatives she is expected to choose fearlessly on the side of life. No price is too high for the vital person to pay, even if the irony of life demands that one chooses the right to life.[8]

Whether it is Major Barbara, Candida or Ann Whitefield, all are duty-bound to life and fulfil nature's purpose of the creation of superman. They are the flesh-and-blood representatives of the Life Force. Shaw's insight behind the attraction between man and woman made Desmond MacCarthy remark that Shaw

> ...attempted to reveal the underlying nature of a passionate mutual attraction between a particular man and a particular woman.... As the great German pessimist, Schopenhaur, had also interpreted it [love, attraction] namely as the will of the race expressing itself through the desires of the individual and often contrary to his or her happiness.... As an individual she is excellently drawn. Instinct leads her to mark down Tanner as the father of her future children...but her deeper instincts—and through these, according to Shaw, the Life Force works-leads her to refuse him [Octavius—the poetical, chivalrous, romantic, idealiser of women] as a husband; the poetic temperament is barren—the Life Force passes it by.[9]

On the other hand is Tanner, who, in spite of his flat refusal and foreknowledge of Ann's real nature, comes in the "Grip of Life Force." He couldn't escape Ann's "liquid" and "ensnaring" eyes and ultimately his "head is in the lioness' mouth." Tanner's perception about Ann has a different stance contrary to Octavius's. He calls her "Boa constrictor" "lioness," "cat," "ironclad" pursuing and hunting for men:

> TANNER. ...she'll commit every crime a respectable woman can; and she'll justify everyone of them by saying that it was the wish of her guardians. She'll put everything on us; and we shall have no more control over her than a couple of mice over a cat.[10] (Act I)

He perceives her trickery and unscrupulousness to win over all the people around her, "...Ann keeps on saying that of course she's only an orphan.... That's the latest game. An Orphan! Its like hearing an iron clad talk about being at the mercy of the wind and waves."[11] (Act I) He has always been reluctant to be her guardian. Tanner's idea of womanish charm and sympathy is "that's the devilish side of a woman's fascination she makes you will your own destruction."[12] (Act I) Tanner expresses the real nature of Ann:

> ...she is a liar. And since she has plunged Tavy head over ears in love with her without any intention of marrying him, she is a coquette, according to the standard definition of a coquette as a woman who rouses passions she has no intention of gratifying.... She is a bully as well. She cannot bully men as she bullies women; so she habitually and unscrupulously uses her personal fascination to make men give her whatever she wants....[13] (Act IV)

But ultimately Ann is victorious in her purpose of prospective father of superman as she gets victory over Tanner, and he realises it and says to her "I love you. The Life Force enchants me: I have the whole world in my arms when I clasp you."[14] (Act IV) Despite a deep knowledge of philosophy of life he is trapped and becomes a mediator between nature and woman.

All the terms and epithets used by the dramatist to denote Ann, in a sense, give negative meaning to her character; while describing her traits and personality Shaw writes that the weaker of her own sex sometimes call her a "cat."[15] At another place describing Violet he writes that Violet is "not a siren, like Ann."[16] Such phrases like "Boa Constrictor" and "Lady Mephistopheles" evoke a degrading and denigrating feeling towards Ann. On the other hand he calls her "Everywoman" and "one of the vital geniuses.... She is a perfectly respectable, perfectly self-controlled woman, and looks it." (Act I) Is "Everywoman" like Ann a combination and amalgamation of vital genius and cat-like unscrupulousness? Does "Everywoman" beguile then like Ann? It means Shaw has this feeling that almost everywoman tries to beguile man by her charm and decorous, modest manners although he has sublimated Life Fore that it fulfils its purpose through women. As mentioned earlier Barbara Bellow Watson commenting on this aspect of Ann's character writes, "Although Shaw acknowledges that every woman is not Ann. Yet Ann is Everywoman in the sense that she does what women commonly would like to do, her success is due in large part to the fact that she is unashamed."[17] "Unashamed" in the sense that she articulates her own desires very adroitly in the name of mother or father or uncle. Regarding this unashamed proclamation of her choice Gareth Griffith in *Socialism and Superior Brains* writes:

> In their business dealings women are unscrupulous, Shaw said: No trick is too low, no web too intricate for the determined huntress as she ensnares the man most likely to father superior children.... Her unscrupulousness was the product of her biologically determined duty to ensure the welfare of the race; women must marry because the race must perish without her travail.[18]

And Ann Whitefield, Shaw's "everywoman," conquers Tanner who finds himself "in the grip of the Life Force" and utters "Ann looks happy; but she is only triumphant, successful, victorious."[19] (Act IV)

Ann has lots of paradoxical elements. Sometimes she plays the role of a morale booster beloved of Octavius and an innocent, stubborn adamant beloved of Tanner. If her intention and ulterior motive is to marry Tanner why she knowingly coaxes Octavius into believing that she loves him. She is a modern woman as she speaks her ardent passion of possessing Tanner and works accordingly but she does it not with conviction and courage rather cunningly and deliberately practising on men's instincts. She herself admits:

> ANN. ...I have a great respect for Violet. She gets her own way always.

> OCTAVIUS [sighing] so do you.
>
> ANN. Yes; but somehow she gets it without coaxing—without having to make people sentimental about her.[20] (Act IV)

Ann does not deceive herself unlike conventional women who deceive themselves to prove others their own truthfulness. She is a hypocrite as far as her dalliance and flirtations with Tanner and Octavius is concerned but she is not a hypocrite to herself, to her own whims and desires. She remains true to herself and far from being prudish and self-sacrificing for the hypocrisies of society which always set the self sacrificing womanly woman on a high pedestal. She wins what she wants. She understands the magic she casts on others and says "what a queer creature you are, Tavy there is no such thing as a willing man when you really go for him [she laughs naughtily]..."[21] (Act IV)

There is much of criticism levelled against the portrait of Ann, Gareth Griffith writes:

> Feminists have abhorred the portrait of Ann and the attendant theory of the mother-women which, among other things, seems to confirm the traditional view of man's superior capacity for abstract thought.[22]

About Shaw's concept of mother-woman Lady Rhondda writes, "[Mother Woman] was the product not of nature but of her environment." As for Ann, "she is a hypocrite, sneak, a cad of the very first water."[23] For this Shaw could not respond to his critics convincingly; he writes, "Ann is of course a cad but it was not qua cad that I called her Everywoman, but as man huntress and slave of nature."[24]

Basically Shaw's interest in Eugenics is more intense in this play. He has evolved a political dimension of sexual relation and has transformed into practical race-welfare and not ethics. Gareth Griffith writes:

> ...in *Man and Superman* where his interest in Eugenics was especially intense, he noted there was a political aspect to the sex question. He claimed in fact that the initiative in sex transactions is politically the most

> important of all the initiatives, because our political experiment of democracy, the last refuge of cheap misgovernment, will ruin us if our citizens are ill bred.[25]

Thus his theory of mother-woman is Shaw's hopeful response to despairing view of progress in this period. Women's contribution to "the life force's pursuit of progress would be the result of their own pursuit of the well-bred male."[26]

There is also emotional lacuna between Tanner and Ann. As Eric Bentley writes:

> There seems no such organic relation between Tanner and Ann as there is between Vivie and her mother, Eliza and Higgins, Candida and Morel.... Tanner and Ann draw no sparks from each other.... There is no relationship at all except that she insists on having him and he cannot evade her successfully because the author won't let him. In this case, we have either to conclude that Frank Harris's kind of criticism applies—or that this is "drama of ideas" and we must not ask it to be otherwise.[27]

Raina, in *Arms and the Man,* is a highly romantic girl and is always lost in her dreams of "higher love." She is introduced as "a young lady, intensively conscious of the romantic beauty of the night and of the fact that her own youth and beauty are part of it..."[28] (Act I) She is always engrossed in her reverie whether it is about romantic love or her romantic illusion of war. Through Raina, Bernard Shaw wants to unwrap the romantic illusions which have covered disastrous wars and unhappy marriages. War and marriage, one is bad and the other is good, have a layer of superficial ideals which ultimately lead to disastrous ends in both the cases. All these romantic ideals get shattered with a stroke of reality in the course of the play. Initially in the play she is very childish but gradually gets transformed. According to Margery M. Morgan:

> She [Raina] is in an obvious sense the most childish character in the play, but this does not prevent her from being Bluntschli's aptest pupil and making the transition from nursery to marriage, ignorance to wisdom, spoilt infancy to maturity, with painless ease.[29]

"Child" Raina gets the news of a victorious Sergius and experiences ecstasy. She thinks that Sergius "the hero of the hour, the idol of the regiment" is higher and greater than her and she does not deserve him. The following conversation gives a glimpse into her love-ridden soul.

> RAINA. Tell me, tell me, How was it? (Ecstatically) Oh, mother! mother! mother! (she pulls her mother down on the ottoman; and they kiss one another frantically).... What will he care for my poor little worship after the acclamations of a whole army of heroes? But no matter: I am so happy! So proud! (she rises and walks about excitedly). It proves that all our ideas were real after all.[30] (Act I)

Raina's "ideals" of "Patriotism" and "heroic ideals" come true with the thumping victory of Sergius and proves him in the eye of Raina a real hero so much so that she belittles herself "Oh, what faithless little creatures girls are!" (Act I) she sets Sergius on the high pedestal and resumes her confidence in her ideal:

> RAINA (laughing and snuggling against her mother) Yes: I was only a prosaic little coward. Oh, to think that it was all true! that Sergius is just as splendid and noble as he looks! that the world is really a glorious world for women who can see its glory and men who can act its romance! What happiness! what unspeakable fulfilment![31] (Act I)

Commenting on the romantic attitude and posture of Raina, Purdom writes:

> When the play opens, and Raina is standing at the window gazing at the snowy Balkans, her reverie is concentrated upon her hero, which means that her pose as she stands and her first speech when she answers her mother must be on the fervent romantic level, not that of comedy, certainly not of naturalism...[32]

Raina exhibits "higher love" not only in her thought process but with her gestures, gesticulations and code of conduct with Sergius. She always gets excited listening to Sergius's heroic deeds.

She even talks to herself about Sergius, "Oh, I shall never be unworthy of you any more, my soul's hero: never, never."[33] (Act I) She puts on "most genteel society manner," and walks with "studied elegance."

In the first part of the play we see Raina as a completely love-ridden girl with high ideals of romance which she exhibits in her relationship with Sergius, her "hero". While in the later part of the play Raina becomes an ordinary girl with practical and real love, stripped off its illusions which she experiences in her relationship with Bluntschli, "the man of the midnight adventure in Raina's room." (Act II) Bluntschli is a soldier whose professional and prosaic approach shatters high ideals of Raina and drags her to the reality, maturing her concept of love. The purpose of Shaw in introducing Bluntschli is the disillusionment of Raina as well as of Sergius. Shaw aimed this play to be an "onslaught on idealism... which is only a flattering name for romance in politics and morals"[34] and the cause of national and personal "moral chaos and anarchy." Explaining this purpose Purdom writes:

> A prosaic professional soldier is introduced into a situation between a typical romantic hero and a typical romantic heroine, with disastrous consequences to both...Shaw's aim is to destroy illusions, and to compel his audience to face realities.[35]

Because to Shaw:

> The tragedy and comedy of life lie in the consequences, sometimes terrible, sometimes ludicrous, of our persistent attempt to found our institutions on the ideals suggested to our imaginations by our half-satisfied passions, instead of on a genuinely scientific natural history.[36]

The relationship of Raina and Sergius is the relationship of "a couple of grown up babies." (Act III) Raina does not want to show meanness, smallness in the presence of Sergius. She cannot even imagine of deceiving Sergius. She says to Bluntschli, "...I want to be quite perfect with Sergius: no meanness, no smallness, no deceit. My relationship to him is the one really beautiful and noble part of my life...."[37] (Act III) She dreams of a consummate relationship with Sergius. Her conversation with Sergius gives a true picture of two romantic souls:

> SERGIUS. Dearest: all my deeds have been yours. You inspired me. I have gone through the war like a knight in a tournament with his lady looking down at him!
>
> RAINA. And you have never been absent from my thoughts for a moment. (Very solemnly) Sergius: I think we two have found the higher love. When I think of you, I feel that I could never do a base deed, or think an ignoble thought.
>
> SERGIUS. My lady and my saint! (He clasps her reverently).
>
> RAINA. (returning his embrace) My lord and my - -[38] (Act II)

Raina and Sergius are presented as the apostles of higher love without lacuna and worldly touch. But both of them have another and different side of their love which they feel unconsciously. Raina's protection of Bluntschli and addressing him as "poor little darling" has a different shade of love. Sergius's advances to Louka and feeling guilty of it also shows a different aspect of love.

Raina, inadvertently and unknowingly, harbours a soft corner for Bluntschli from the very beginning. She saves Bluntschli, gives her chocolates to eat. In fact she has a real relationship wherein both of them face attacks and counterattacks. This "conflict of wills" exposes the reality without any demonstration of disguise. In the contact of Bluntschli her "most cherished ideals of manhood" get a blow and she is deeply wounded. She comes to know the difference between professional and unprofessional soldiers. She adores Sergius for being a "hero" and "patriot" but Bluntschli proves him to be a "pretender and a coward." Raina has the very sublime view of her soldiers and her hero but Bluntschli's businesslike attitude and his experience proves her that all are novice and first-timers.

Raina takes Bluntschli into confidence and hides him. After all verbal duels, she promises him and gives her "hand in pledge" of his "security." This is the beginning of trust. When Bluntschli falls asleep in her room she comes with her mother, who tries to wake him up. Raina detains her, "Don't mamma: the poor darling is worn out. Let him sleep." (Act I) Catherine is surprised to listen to this address. She gets amazed and says, "The poor darling! Raina!!" (She looks at her daughter). (Act I) This is the beginning of real love although unintentionally.

In the relationship of Raina and Bluntschli, there is no pretension. Although Raina wears the mask of conceit, vanity, Bluntschli unmasks her. There is the anti-climax of the play conspicuous of Shavian plays, which changes her from "the heroic to a babyish familiarity":

> BLUNTSCHLI. I can't help it. When you strike that boble attitude and speech in that thrilling voice, I admire you, but I find it impossible to believe a single word you say.
>
> RAINA. (standing over him, as if she could not believe her senses) Do you mean what you said just now? Do you know what you said just now?
>
> BLUNTSCHLI. I dc
>
> RAINA. (gasping) I! I!!! (she points to herself incredulously, meaning "I, Raina Petkoff, tell lies!" He meets her gaze unflinchingly. She suddenly sits down beside him, and adds, with a complete change of manner from the heroic to a babyish familiarity). How did you find me out?[39] (Act III)

Raina reveals to him that he is the first man who has not taken Raina seriously. She unveils what everybody has believed "the noble attitude and the thrilling voice" (Act III) since her childhood. This revelation of Raina's real nature does not make Bluntschli despise her, rather he discloses his real intention. He speaks about the nature of Raina "Its part of your youth: part of your charm, I'm like all the rest of them: the nurse, your parents, Sergius: I'm your infatuated admirer."[40] (Act III) Thus Raina gets a romantic command over Bluntschli. Ultimately when she discovers Louka-Sergius relationship she realizes the real love and recognises "hollow sham" of love. At last Raina succumbs to her "chocolate cream soldier," who cures her of the deception of romantic notion of love and war which rules her life when the play begins. She no longer has the concept of war as a romantic game and marriage as the union of a pretty heroine and a handsome brave, courageous hero in an everlasting romantic dream. Instead of pretentious, fickle-minded Sergius she takes plain and prosaic Bluntschli as her husband, giving her stability and comfort. She gets mature when she asserts, "Next time, I hope you will know the difference between a school girl of seventeen and a woman of twenty three." (Act III)

Shaw's idea of taking two couples—Raina Sergius and Louka Bluntschli and causing them to exchange partners after a conflict and disparity in their mindset serves a hidden purpose. The purpose is that seemingly comfortable coexistence may turn out to be deceptive and hypocritical. Raina passes over from Sergius's world to that of Bluntschli. Conflict and clash prepare the ground for real relationship. Norbert F. O'Donnell in his article "The Conflict of Wills in Shaw's Tragic Comedy" writes about the relevance of strife and rift in relations and says:

> The moments of true feeling which are the basis of the Shavian tragicomedy emerge naturally from the conflicts which provide the psychological undercurrents of the plays. They may be distinguished as moments of "nakedness," moments of "disillusionment," and moments of "conversion"—each reflecting a character's defeat or victory in the struggle of wills.[41]

Raina experiences "moments of nakedness" and wins at last descending to the level of her "chocolate cream soldier."

The action of the play is initially the development of Raina as a woman: and according to Valency, Shaw's identification is more with the women of his plays than with the male characters, not that he had a deeper insight into the mind of his female protagonists. "From a psychological viewpoint it would seem that it is in Raina that Shaw prefigured his innermost self, his ego, poised somewhat precariously between the conflicting elements of his nature."[42]

> His women fall into rather obvious molds. Masterful women of the type of Lady Cicely or Candida impressed him most. He had a vivid impression of the sort of sexless

> spinster represented by Vivie Warren. But women normally of passionate nature seem to have inspired him mainly with fear and therefore showed clear traces of the vampire. The most manageable women in his canon were those who are amenable to the tutelage of a masterful male. These generally resulted in delightful characterisations. The suggestion is therefore tempting that the education of Raina, as well as that of Cleopatra, Eliza, Barbara, and Ellie Dunn represents in some sense the education of Shaw.[43]

Eliza Doolittle a "flower girl" is the central character in the play *Pygmalion*. Phonetics is the mainstay of the play, but it deals ultimately with human relations and emotion especially love and affection. Prof. Higgins, a philosopher scientist, is forty years old. He is the author of *Higgins Universal Alphabet*. He claims to have the ability to make anyone learn any dialect and the art of speaking eloquently. For his "scientific experiment," he fortunately meets Eliza who wants to be a lady in a flower shop but is unable to get the hold of it due to her cockney accent. She wants to learn more "genteel" language. Higgins employs his "Miltonic Mind" to represent her as a "duchess" and he succeeds in his attempts of transforming a common, "flower girl" into a "duchess" and a "princess". Eliza, in the meantime, falls in love with her mentor, a heartless and stonehearted man who has the least expectation of it. Expressing the same thought Purdom writes: "A philosopher scientist creates an image that falls in love with him, and what to him is a scientific experiment turns out to be an exercise in the natural affection of the human heart."[44]

Eliza has been portrayed as a woman to the core, conscious of her womanly feelings and passions, but Higgins is an intellectual personality, devoid of all humanity and softer feelings. He has no interest in any woman. He himself admits "...the moment I let myself make friends with a woman, I become selfish and tyrannical."[45] (Act II) Women cannot enchant and enthral him. "I've taught scores of American millionairesses how to speak English: the best looking women in the world. I'm seasoned. They might as well be blocks of wood. I might as well be a block of wood...."[46] (Act II) Higgins is a true stoic, a devoted and professional professor, "a confirmed old bachelor." (Act II) So the conflict between head (Higgins) and heart (Eliza) is apparently rational. As Purdom has also expressed:

> Eliza is a true woman, a natural romantic type. Conflict between the two on the level of unconscious comedy-romance makes the play. Higgins belongs to the intellect, she has no mind at all; he has not discovered his heart, she is nothing but heart; he sees her for exactly what she is, but does not know himself.[47]

The story of *Pygmalion* is the story of "making a woman." Eliza, conscious of her virtues and immaculate character since the inception, utters "I am a good girl" (Act II) whenever she has the least suspicion of people taking her in a wrong way. She devotes herself completely to her creator in order to be a perfect creation. She gets the desired result and proves successful in her pursuit of being a duchess. Eliza goes through a transformation of inner soul in the process of learning to become a duchess. She has deep-rooted feminine instincts and always conforms to this instinct. While creating the character of Eliza, Shaw had in his mind Cinderella's fairly tale and the Pygmalion Myth. Figuratively Cinderella connotes a girl who having faced the traumatic life, gets ultimate bliss. Eliza also spends a poverty-ridden and stringent life for a long time and ultimately reaches the zenith like Cinderella. Her education in phonetics, her training in middle class manners and morality transform her from a flower girl to a duchess. Another synthesis in the character of Eliza is that of Galatea, the sweetheart of Pygmalion legend in Greek mythology. Galatea was an ivory statue of a girl created by Pygmalion, the sculptor. She was an ideal image of beauty and her creator falls in love with her. By the animating grace of Aphrodite, that ivory statue became a moving flesh and blood girl and reciprocated the love of her architect. Eliza, a flower girl like the ivory statue of Galatea, undergoes a rigorous training to become a perfect woman. She also turns out to be a real duchess, not by birth but by manners and has an eloquent speaking style. Higgins, like Pygmalion, trains her in phonetics and makes her learn social behaviour in order to make her a perfect lady and to survive with middle class morality.

Shaw has inculcated these two mythical stories but in parts only; Eliza's character and personality have been raised above these two. In the mythical stories both the images Cinderella and Galatea are like dolls. They take the steps that they are destined to take and ultimately get married to the objects of their choice or we can say that they get their creators as their lovers. Whereas Eliza raises herself from the common romanticism of life to the status of a full mature woman and then takes decision. One critic has envisaged the same idea, "Eliza's progress is a sort of spiritual voyage from darkness to light. She achieves final personal fulfilment through successive stages of inspiration, purgation, illumination and despair."[48]

Eliza goes through these stages of "purgation, illumination and despair" in her relation with Prof. Higgins. In her efforts to learn the sophisticated speech of sophisticated people, she devotes herself to her master. She brings his slippers, makes all types of arrangements even buying and selling from markets. When Prof. Higgins succeeds in his pursuit of presenting Eliza as a duchess in the community, he gets satisfaction and complacence with his efforts. He does not pay heed to Eliza's work and this indifference to her sincerity makes her rebel against him. This is the moment when Eliza crosses her doll-like projection. She goes beyond fetching slippers and doing other household chores. It is not only Prof. Higgins's diligent and persistent efforts but also Eliza's unflinching devotion to her master which makes the accomplishment possible. Louis Crompton's comments elaborate this aspect:

> He [Higgins] and Pickering alike have both failed to grasp the fact that Eliza's heroic efforts to improve herself...are first of all the result of a doglike devotion to two masters who have taken trouble over her. When the men fail to pet and admire her after her triumph, her thwarted feelings turn to rage, and desperate to provoke an emotional response from Higgins, she needles him so she may enjoy the spectacle of a god in a vulgar human fury.[49]

Despite being successful as a duchess in the eyes of others, Eliza is the same flower girl to Higgins. It really wounds her when she realizes that Higgins takes her as an experimental object without sentiments and feelings. She does not receive the treatment which she deserves. One critic has written:

> From Eliza's viewpoint, however, the difference between a flower girl is not how she behaves, but how she is treated. Her experience is that apart from the things anyone can pick up (the dressing and the proper way of speaking, and so on) what gives estimation to a person is the attitude of the person to whom he or she is related.[50]

Higgins is a typical Shavian character who takes everything intellectually not physically or emotionally. His relation with Eliza is at the cerebral level. He tells Eliza that he cares for "humanity." Higgins's domineering superiority causes Eliza to rebel against him. Eliza's development takes place when she understands the bullying nature of Higgins. Shaw has written about Eliza "Eliza has no use for the foolish romantic tradition that all women love to be mastered, if not actually bullied and beaten."[51]

Higgins is devoid of humanity of his creation. He does not comprehend the responsibility of a creator, Louis Crompton writes:

> Higgins is in many ways a paradoxical being. He is at once a tyrannical bully and a charmer, an impish schoolboy and a flamboyant wooer of souls, a scientist with a wildly extravagant imagination and a man so blind to the nature of his own personality that he thinks of himself as timid, modest and difficult.[52]

The influence of Higgins's mother on him leaves him unaffectionate to other women. Shaw has written:

> Higgins excused his indifference to young women on the ground that they had an irresistible rival in his mother.... If an imaginative boy has a sufficiently rich mother who has intelligence, personal grace, dignity of character without harshness, and a cultivated sense of the best art of her time to enable her to make her house beautiful, she sets a standard for him against which very few women can struggle...[53]

Thus Higgins has idealized his mother instead of Eliza. It emphasises the importance of mother in Higgins' life. When he already has an ideal woman favouring him he does not need another woman. It is also true that Higgins is fond of Eliza involuntarily, but he never treats Eliza as Galatea, sweet-heart of Pygmalion. Eliza's relationship with Higgins is dehumanised relation: a relationship of cold hearted professor and a student which she realizes later on and acts instinctively and accordingly. She repudiates the notion that all women want to be mastered and asserts her own individuality. She wants natural love not somebody to bully her. She understands the wretchedness of being an experimental object. We can say Professor Higgins's denial hurts her but makes her a woman of the world, an emotionally balanced woman which was the main aim of Professor. Higgins is Shaw's mouthpiece who encourages all the women to stand by themselves.

Critics have analysed Eliza as a vulgar, physical girl who belongs to herself only, not to the race of "world betterer." As Crompton comments: "She has nothing of the impersonality of the world betterer, nothing of Higgins's scientific passion for reform."[54] Higgins belongs to humanity not to any individual. People of high culture always seem to be cold and unaffectionate to all human and commonplace people. So is the case with Eliza and Higgins.

Through Eliza Shaw has made a successful effort to project the manners, behaviour, social etiquettes of middle class people. When Eliza hires a taxi and goes to Higgins she feels proud of it, because flower girls were not permitted to hire taxis. Didactically the transformation of Eliza shows the effect of environment and ambience on an individual and his/her social behaviour. Environment is the factor which moulds a personality and gives it colour. Eliza's success shows that only speech is the barrier in social stratum which shows the difference of society. Through Eliza Shaw shows that the training of "middle class manners," "education in phonetics" are important factors to survive in a sophisticated society.

We can also see Shaw's anti-romanticism in the play. Shaw has synthesized myth and fancy in a beautiful way giving it a slight turn. When everybody expects a romantic end to the story of Eliza and Higgins, Shaw, following the theory of Life-Force, makes

Higgins super-human, immaculate and free of carnal and worldly desires. Eliza, having got maturity of thoughts, gets married to Freddy in order to maintain the theory of Life Force. C.E.M. Joad writes:

> ...She feels and acts in this way because of the impulsion of the Life Force which expresses in her as a persistent drive to maintain and conserve life at the level which it has already reached and to keep it smoothly functioning at that level. New Men like Higgins don't want mothering and reassuring...[55]

It is for this reason that Eliza chooses Freddy Hill as her marriage partner. Speaking about the man of her destiny she says: "And if he's weak and poor and want me may be he'd make me happier than my betters that bully me and don't want me." (Act IV) Thus Shaw wants to show the dominating part of the "woman motif" in the lives of "common" and "ordinary" men. In the words of C.E.M. Joad "she exhibits herself as a consistent exponent of Shaw's philosophy."[56]

Eliza has been viewed as a prostitute indirectly by many a critic, although there is no physical relationship and there is a disentanglement of sex relations. A.M. Gibbs writes:

> The analogy between Eliza's situation and that of a prostitute has been lightly insinuated from very near the beginning of her progress towards becoming a lady, when Higgins buys her from her father, Doolittle, for five pounds. Until the last scene of the play Eliza is in a position of economic, as well as emotional and intellectual, dependence on Higgins. She is kept woman.[57]

Eliza might be in love with Higgins as Shaw has written in its sequel:

> She has even secret mischievous moments in which she wishes she could get him alone, on a desert island, away from all ties and with nobody else in the world to consider, and just drag him off his pedestal and see him making love like any common man. We all have private imaginations of that sort.[58]

But when it comes to the realities of life she forsakes dreamy and fanciful life and becomes the lady love of Freddy. Shaw has written, "Galatea never does quite like Pygmalion: his relation to her is too godlike to be altogether agreeable."[59]

At last we can say in the words of A.M. Gibbs, "*Pygmalion* is a play about the pupil's regaining, through struggle, of her identity and independence."[60] This is an odyssey of identity and freedom for Eliza and she travels successfully, she turns into a mature woman from an immature, vulgarly hysterical girl. When Eliza says that she no longer needs him she can do without him, Higgins, in high spirits, speaks "By George Eliza, I said I'd make a woman of you; and I have.... Five minutes ago you were like a millstone round my neck. Now you're a tower of strength; a consort battleship."[61] (Act V) We can quote here Norbert F. O' Donnell to show that Eliza has the accountability of transforming herself into a fearless human being who drags her master to the level of a common man however great he may be. He writes:

> Liza Doolittle is transformed from a subhuman flower girl into a truly human being because she shakes off her fears, develops a will of her own, and is able to meet Higgins as an equal in the strife of wills which is human condition.... Her final transformation takes place only when she asserts purposes of her own which are not born of intimidation, knocking Higgins off the god-like perch from which he has viewed her only as an object, awakening for the first time his anger and his genuine human concern for her. The "squashed cabbage leaf" becomes, as Higgins puts it, a "consort battleship." The military metaphor is significant, Liza is fully human because she is now prepared to engage on equal terms with Higgins in a warfare of wills.[62]

Hypatia is the central character in the play *Misalliance*. She is "a striking, dark, purposeful, handsome young woman, longing for she does not know what." In fact her passion for something unknown or mysterious keeps her on her toes and renders the play a subtle meaning. Commenting on this element of mystery Purdom writes, "The real difficulty is with Hypatia, who must convey mystery, the mystery of the female mind, yet not a mere calculating creature: she is a poetic creation."[63] "The mystery of the female mind" is the major aspect of the play which is explored in different ways in different women.

Hypatia is a marriageable girl but she is desirous of marrying not for love but for something to happen. She is Bentley's fiancée, proposes and provokes Mr. Percival to make love to her. Her actions and words symbolise the deep recesses of female mind. Through her actions she raises many questions which make her character enigmatic and controversial. Her romantic initiative, despite being betrothed, raises the question of emancipation, freedom from sexual, mental and social limitations and inhibitions. Is it an advance form of feminism wherein a woman has the absolute right to express her innermost desires as a man has?

Hypatia has a matter-of-fact and down-to-earth attitude towards men and marriage. She is ready to marry "cry-baby" Bentley because she has no better choice. She tells her mother that most of the men are either handsome, have an attractive body or have only brains; no man is born with both the qualities. In this regard she would prefer to have Bentley since he has all the brains, no matter if he is not able bodied and is not well-built. She says "Not one of them (boys) has as much brains in his whole body as Bentley has in his little finger.... He may be small but he's the best of the bunch. You can not deny that."[64] Thus she is scraping the bottom of the barrel. She doesn't love Bentley yet readies to marry him.

Love does not attract Hypatia instead she is apprehensive of getting married to an object of love. She frankly asserts that she would not risk marrying a man for love. She has the opinion that to marry a man whom a woman loves makes that woman a "perfect slave." Hypatia here reiterates Grace's answer in *The Philanderer*. She thinks that a girl should marry a man who loves that girl. In fact Hypatia's quest for her Mr. Perfect is not fulfilled so she lives in a dream world and imagines him to be with her. Her groom-hunting gets over towards the end of the play with the arrival of Joey Percival. She says, "I can imagine all sorts of men I could fall in love with; but I never seem to meet them. The real ones are too small, like Bunny, or too silly, like Jerry."[65] Bunny or Bentley is Hobson's choice for her as there is no alternative.

Hypatia is in dilemma because she does not get intelligence, brain and good body together in one man. J.L. Wisenthal writes about her disposition that this "opposition between body and brain" has been referred to many times in the course of the play. Hypatia contrasts Bentley with her other suitors. She describes Jerry, her former suitor, as a "splendid animal" but a foolish person. "She must choose between brainless matter and immaterial brain, and she wants both mental and physical distinction in a husband."[66]

Hypatia's treatment of Bentley is that of a mother towards a baby. She enters the play protecting Bentley from her brother as if he were a baby. She herself reveals it to her mother, that she is fond of him. This aspect of infantilisation of a grown up man is one of the rampant traits of women in Shavian plays. Candida also spoonfeeds Morell as if he were a child, calling him a "baby."

Hypatia feels frustration in her home where there is nothing but talks and talks only. She is fed up with the surfeit of talk and ideas and wants to be an "active verb." She experiences that all social conventions bind a woman and crush her sensibilities:

> Oh, I daresay it's vulgar; but there's no other word for it. I'm fed up with nice things: with respectability, with propriety! When a woman has nothing to do, money and respectability mean that nothing is ever allowed to happen to her. I don't want to be good; and I don't want to be bothered about either good or bad: I want to be an active verb.[67]

Woman should have respectability with propriety, all these nice things are repellent to her because these do not give her freedom. She says that she wants to be independent of the assumption of "good" or "bad." A woman is reduced to the status of a nursing maid suffering and sacrificing for others. She says, "Girls withering into ladies. Ladies withering into old maids. Nursing old women. Running errands for old men. Good for nothing else at last."[68] She asserts that she abhors family, "Oh, home! home! parents! family! duty! how I loathe them! How I'd like to see them all blown to bits!...."[69] She ultimately desires to be "wicked."

Actually Hypatia is very much dissatisfied with the environment she lives in, as a mere passive object, she wants "something to happen" which is a symbol of her perpetual quest for something mysterious. She says that she would prefer to put up with swearing and smoking than with dull respectability. Tarleton, her father, is very well aware of her mysterious disposition; he says that she is not satisfied and is always restless. She wants adventures to drop out of the sky.

Certainly Hypatia's search for unknown is over as soon as her father's allusion to adventure dropping out of the sky comes true with an aircraft taking a nosedive. Here begins Hypatia's chase for Joey Percival who lands with the aircraft. Her "wild impulses" and desire to be a "glorious young beast" get full-fledged expression and exposure before this Greek god Percival, Whom she tells: "Nobody else ever called me a glorious young beast. I like that. Glorious young beast expresses exactly what I like to be."[70]

Hypatia-Percival relationship gives the impression of Ann-Tanner relationship. Hypatia, like Ann, initiates lovemaking. She continuously chases Percival and instigates him to do with her what he wishes. He tries to escape from her unsuccessfully like Tanner and at last gets trapped. The interaction between Hypatia and Percival unveils the true colours of both the persons. The conduct of both the persons are interchanged. Percival behaves and tries to protect himself as if he were a girl. Hypatia tries to pounce upon him like an animal on its prey. She openly and frankly invites him, "... come, handsome young man, and play with the respectable shopkeeper's daughter.... You may kiss me if you catch me."[71] Commenting on this animal like impulses J.L. Wisenthal writes:

> She is a classic example of the Shavian Philistine, and, as with Ann Whitefield in *Man and Superman*, her primitive motivation is suggested by the repeated mention of animals in connection with her.... In her approach to Joey Percival she fulfils admirably this ideal [of being a 'beast'] which she has set up for herself.[72]

Her repetition of the phrases "How I envy the animals," "brute," "wicked" expresses definitely her psychology. When she takes initiative in her pursuit of love towards Percival, the stage direction describes her actions which are similar to that of a predatory animal—"Hypatia, excited, mischievous, her eyes glowing, runs in, precisely on his trail."[73] Later she, in search of Percival, chases him out in the woods when he becomes pursuer she "fights like a wild cat." Michael Holroyd calls it "the biological method of serving the Life Force."[74] When she coaxes her father into getting him, her demand is "Papa: buy the brute for me" J.L. Wisenthal catches the implication that this demand comprises "two Philistine concerns" of "sex and money" as in *Man and Superman*.[75]

Hypatia scolds Percival for retreating in lady-like way and taking support of traditions and norms of society. She reproaches him and attacks him like a man as soon as he addresses her as Miss Tarleton:

> O man! Mean, stupid, cowardly, selfish masculine male man! You ought to have been a governess. I was expelled from school for saying that the very next person that said "Really Miss Tarleton!" to me, I would strike across the face. You were the next.[76]

Her comment about her independence from social conventions also gives an insight into her true soul—"Men like conventions because men made them. I did not make them: I don't like them."[77] It gives a moral shock to the stranger gunner hidden in Turkish bath who eventually exclaims "The men effeminate, the women unsexed."[78]

There is only love-chase between Hypatia and Percival and there is no real love between them. Writing about this lack of romance and real love Maurice Valency writes, "In his desire to minimize the romantic, Shaw makes Hypatia's acquisition of Joey Percival a purely mercantile operation. There is much talk of love between them, but no love."[79]

Hypatia's striking Percival reminds us of Blanche Sartorius who strikes her servant in *Widowers Houses* and Julia Craven in *The Philanderer* who strikes Charteris. Hypatia uses swear words and slang language for which her mother scolds her. Her overt invitation to Percival for making love to her, her desire to be a beast are certainly some of the characteristics of New Woman at that time. It is also true that Shaw's New Women are somewhat manly in their thinking, approach towards others. Is this imitation of male habits a form of feminism? Might be so because it was the first step towards emancipation where woman starts behaving like man to show more or less equality. As Tarleton says, "We are all human: males and females of the same species. When the dress is the same the distinction vanishes."[80]

Hypatia is quite convincingly a dominating love chaser. One who loves neither Bentley nor Percival. She is fascinated by the idea of loving a perfect man who has intelligence as well as charismatic and attractive personality. Percival is also not in love with her rather fascinated by her.

The Philanderer is the second of Shaw's unpleasant plays. Thematically it deals with human emotions of love, jealousy and social institution of marriage; it is a satirical comic piece on the Victorian values and displays the war of love between male and female sexes; their theoretical and practical assumptions about love and marriage. According to Purdom, love and marriage has been "treated as a game between the sexes, within a highly unpleasant fantasia upon Victorian standards; for beneath its playfulness sex is given the serious treatment."[81]

The play was written in the eighteen-nineties when Ibsenism was influencing the whole society as well as literature. In the Prefatory Note of 1930 to *The Philanderer* Shaw wrote about the play that since it was a "topical" play it had become dated. However, he very strongly and categorically refused to update it, his line of defence being—"The human nature in it is still in the latest fashion."[82] He further commented "life itself was staggering from the impact of Ibsen's plays, which reached us in 1889. The state of mind represented by the Ibsen club in this was familiar then to our Intelligentsia."[83] The whole ambience of the play is replete with the doctrines of Ibsen and the fashionable cult of Ibsenism and 'New Womanism' has pervaded the play. This recurrent influence of Ibsen expresses the changing attitudes towards the relations of the sexes and complexity of the struggle for emancipation from imprisoning sexual roles. *The Philanderer* takes up this volatile and variable attitude towards the traditional concept of sex roles.

Grace Tranfield, Julia Craven and her sister Sylvia Craven are the leading women characters who personify the avant-garde values of an Ibsen-influenced society.

Grace Tranfield is a widow "about 32, slight of build, delicate of feature, and sensitive in expression...show plenty of determination."[84] She reflects all the virtues and qualities of a New Woman. Desmond MacCarthy calls her "a preliminary study for the superior women the dramatist afterwards drew."[85] However, we shall discuss Grace as a perfect new woman (as Shaw thought her to be) in chapter IV of the thesis.

Another important female figure is Julia Craven, "beautiful, dark, tragic-looking, passionate, unscrupulous,...a charmer of men."[86] She is introduced as "charming" and "dangerous" to Charteris. Julia, in her relationship with the Philanderer and Casanova Charteris, does not attain maturity, nevertheless she learns the futility of her love and her being a "plaything" not a "companion" for Charteris. That eventual realisation of being nothing makes no effect on Julia. She remains the same childish, jealous bully.

The play examines the emotions of love and makes an effort to discover real love in pursuit of Charteris by these two women: Julia and Grace. Julia and Grace symbolise two different types of women with their own idiosyncrasies. Julia is a jealous termagant who bullies and fights Grace to win Charteris.

Julia's first appearance on the stage presents her as an aggressive woman, as a battle-axe. As she gets the view of Charteris and Grace sitting together she struggles furiously with Charteris to attack Grace and unable to do so, she strikes Charteris in the face as she frees herself. Julia professes to be an "advanced woman" who regards "marriage as a degrading bargain, by which a woman sells herself to a man for the social status of a wife and the right to be supported and pensioned in old age out of his income."[87]

As a member of Ibsen club and a broad minded new woman, Julia does not have faith in the institution of marriage and she reserves the right to leave Charteris at any time if she discovers their companionship incompatible with her full development as a human being. As the play deals with passion of love on its deeper significance, Julia displays the sincerity of that passion. Her feeling of love is of paramount importance. As A.M. Gibbs in *The Art And Mind of Shaw* has written:

Despite her melodramatic posturing and obsessiveness, Julia displays a seriousness and intensity of passion which presents a significant challenge to the theorists of the Ibsen Club. Her very unreasonableness is an index of her humanity: 'I'm too miserable to argue—to think, she tells Charteris, 'I only know I love you.'[88]

Julia is more susceptible than Grace or any other character in the play. It is her susceptibility and her extraordinary capacity for feeling that projects her the most vulnerable character. In an extreme fit of jealousy she behaves like a child and her action makes her the "most sympathetic character."[89] Although she proclaims to be an unwomanly woman yet she turns out to be a womanly woman. "A tigress over her cub" turns out to be "the family baby." Why does Julia behave like a spoilt baby? It is because she realises the passion of love more than anybody else does. This extremity has been the result of a feeling of loneliness in Julia and it is making her feel that she is all alone in this big wide world. She thinks that nobody loves her and cares for her. Nobody tries to understand the real nature of Julia except Paramore who understands her very well and says, "It is your heart, your sincerity, your sterling reality, your great gifts of character that are only half developed because you have never been understood by those around you."[90] (Act III)

Thus behind Julia's peculiar temperament and mentality there is a society and its inhabitants—the society which imposes some rules and regulations on people and makes it necessary for them to behave in a particular, certain way acceptable to society. The Ibsen Club entailed to be manly woman and womanly man for its members. Being a woman, Julia has to show herself as a manly woman or unwomanly woman, while she is every inch a woman. This simulation of being a new, advanced, unwomanly woman affects her badly and negatively. Margery M. Morgan in *The Shavian Playground* comments on the sociological rationale behind Julia's idiosyncratic behaviour and writes:

> Julia Craven, the woman of passion, is hounded down by the author and his deputies to the end of *The Philanderer*, which leaves her looking more of a victim than a villainess. No attempt is made to diagnose the social origins of Julia's emotions: neurotic, hysterical,

> characteristically violent, they challenge the intelligence and the compassion of an audience rather as the spectacle of Hedda Gabler's frustrated and destructive vitality does. Implied in the individual figure is the sickness of a society; but the public aspect of its disease is not admitted to the picture.[91]

Julia has the feeling of insecurity somewhere in her unconscious mind which results in childish tantrums. Writing about this feeling of insecurity Margery M. Morgan says:

> Julia's rages of frustration and jealousy and despair are the signs of a childish helplessness and fear of rejection, the insecurity of a creature who has never learnt independence of others like the spoilt child, Julia has acquired the cunning to use the appeal of her helplessness as a weapon of tyranny over others. Her father's testimony, 'she can't bear to be crossed in the slightest thing, poor child,' is echoed with the severity of a schoolmistress in Grace's accusation: you calculated to an inch how far you could go...you fall back on your natural way of getting anything you want: crying for it like a baby until it is given to you.[92]

Julia has been modelled after Jenny Patterson, one of the friends and pupils of Shaw's mother. In a letter to Frank Harris, Shaw wrote:

> I escaped seduction until I was 29, when an enterprising widow, one of my mother's pupils, appealed successfully to my curiosity. If you want to know what it was, read *The Philanderer*, and cast her for the part of Julia, and me for that of Charteris, I was, in fact, a born Philanderer...[93]

In another letter to Hesketh Pearson, Shaw wrote:

> Mrs. Patterson was my model for Julia; and the first act of *The Philanderer* is founded on a very horrible scene between her and Florence Farr.... [Mrs. Patterson was] an ungovernably jealous woman making violent scenes whenever I spoke to any other woman. She was amazingly jealous, not merely in love but in every other relation in life, regardless of sex.[94]

Julia is one of the early portraits of Shaw's women so she embodies all the qualities of those women who came in contact with Shaw first and foremost. She is not like Candida or any other independent woman nor does she understand any lesson in the end as Raina or Eliza. Gareth Griffith in *Socialism And Superior Brains* writes, "The portraits of women in Shaw's early plays often expressed the complications involved in the process of emancipation."[95] Julia is Shaw's early heroine and through her Shaw has portrayed the womanly woman taking only first step towards her emancipation from the conventional sexual roles. She falls in love with Charteris and claims to have him by hook or by crook. Even Charteris calls her a new woman but in a restricted sense, i.e. Julia is not that sort of woman who, being rejected, hides her emotion or takes refuge in any other form. Rather she expresses her emotional and physical desires violently and overtly. She oversteps the mark in the pursuit of her loving object. Shaw examines the validity of advanced views and satirises against those women who simulate to be New Women through Julia. Observing this implication Desmond MacCarthy says:

> Mr. Shaw sympathised with the woman's movement, as his *Quintessence of Ibsenism* remains to show; but as a critical observer he saw clearly enough that many women who went in for emancipating themselves had not thrown off the 'old' woman when they put on the 'new.' This play is a satire which exposes such women effectively enough.[96]

We must also note what Gareth Griffith has observed:

> Through Julia Shaw portrayed the womanly woman as a huntress, using all her skills of calculated emotion and outrage in her pursuit of Charteris. She was every bit as vituperative and theatrically hysterical in her quest for her stage lover as the flouted Mrs. Patterson was in her search for the elusive Shaw. Julia Craven, as her sir name suggests, was an impostor in the Ibsen Club. She was incapable of conducting an honest and open relationship with men or women; she was the perfect manipulator of the established system, earning high

> praise from the manly man, Cuthbertson: 'A splendid fine creature: every inch a woman. No Ibsenism about her!'[97]

There is a sense of ambiguity in the character of Julia as her own attitude towards herself shows that she is an extremely beautiful woman and all the men like her very much and take her as "a Persian Cat." Commenting on this element of ambiguity A.M. Gibbs writes:

> Her own attitude towards her own sexual attractiveness is ambiguous. She taunts Charteris with the comparative unattractiveness of her rivals for his affection and calls Grace a 'Creature with no figure'; but at the same time sees her own beauty as a barrier in her relations with men.[98]

Grace reproaches Julia for being the woman who degrades all women in the eyes of men by not being a self-respected and self-willed woman:

> 'I' see by you, what wretched childish creatures we are! ...I will not give myself to any man who has learnt how to treat women from you and your like. I can do without his love but not without his respect.[99] (Act II)

Shaw has contrasted Julia, the Victorian "womanly woman" with self complacent Grace Tranfield, her counterpart. Julia is an expansion of Blanche Sartorious, an outrageous lovely woman in *Widowers' Houses*. Desmond MacCarthy calls her the "first sketch of Ann."[100] It is apparent that Julia is not the fully developed New Woman but she has the potential of being one, only if she exercises full control over her emotions. Julia is not accountable for her deplorable situation; it is, in the words of Margery M. Morgan, "that Don Juanism is responsible for women like Julia."[101]

A close examination of a few love-ridden Shavian women unravels Shaw's ulterior motive behind the unprecedented creation of so-called "unashamed" and "selfish" Greek goddesses. In Shaw's viewpoint, the nobility of these mother-women's higher motive negates the unpleasantness of their unscrupulous or promiscuous behaviour. The depiction of eager women and reluctant men in this chapter, as Shaw pointed out artistically and polemically, is the unconscious working of the Life Force. The struggle for supremacy between the mother-women and the artistic men is a fight of similar powers. But if the man happens to be a sublime altruist and an egotist, he is used by the Life Force for different purpose other than the one being searched for by the woman. The latter's quest for Life Fore is for procreation of better human beings; however this female endeavour does not tempt the artistic man, who has different goals before him. Shavian characters like Professor Higgins, Octavius, Marchbanks, Bentley and Shaw himself are some of the examples of such males.

REFERENCES

1. Barbara Bellow Watson, *A Shavian Guide to The Intelligent Woman*, (London: Chatto and Windus, 1964), p. 60.
2. *Ibid*, p, 61.
3. *Ibid*, p, 60.
4. Maurice Valency, *The Cart and The Trumpet: The Plays of George Bernard Shaw*, (New York: Oxford University Press, 1973), p. 109.
5. CB Purdom, *A Guide to the Plays of Bernard Shaw*, (London: University Paperbacks, Methuen, 1963), pp. 195-196.
6. George Bernard Shaw, *Man and Superman*, ed. S. Sengupta, (Delhi: Surjeet Publications, 2000), p. 18.
7. *Ibid*, p. 179.
8. Barbara Bellow Watson, *A Shavian Guide to The Intelligent Woman*, (London: Chatto and Windus, 1964), p. 61.
9. Desmond MacCarthy, *Shaw*, (London: Macgibbon and Kee, 1991), pp. 33-34.
10. *Man and Superman*, pp. 11-12.
11. *Ibid*, pp. 12-13.
12. *Ibid*, p. 26.
13. *Ibid*, pp. 185-186.
14. *Ibid*, p. 193.
15. CB Purdom, *A Guide to the Plays of Bernard Shaw*, p. 198.
16. *Ibid*, p. 199.
17. Barbara Bellow Watson, *A Shavian Guide to The Intelligent Woman*, p. 60.
18. Gareth Griffith, *Socialism and Superior Brains: The Political Thought of Bernard Shaw*, (London: Routledge, 1993), p. 178.

19. *Man and Superman*, p. 196.
20. *Ibid*, p. 182.
21. *Ibid*, p. 180.
22. Gareth Griffith, *Socialism and Superior Brains*: The Political Thought of Bernard Shaw, p. 179.
23. Lady Rhondda (1930s), "Shaw's Women", *Time and Tide* 14 March: 3314 as quoted in Gareth Griffith, *Socialism and Superior Brains: The Political Thought of Bernard Shaw*, p. 179.
24. D.H. Laurence, *Shaw-Collected Letters 1926-1950*, (London: Max Reinhardt, 1988, as quoted in Gareth Griffith, *Socialism and Superior Brains: The Political Thought of Bernard Shaw*, p. 179.
25. Gareth Griffith, *Socialism and Superior Brains: The Political Thought of Bernard Shaw*, p. 179.
26. *Ibid*, p. 179.
27. Eric Bentley, "The Making of a Dramatist (1892-1903)" in *G.B. Shaw: A Collection of Critical Essays*, ed. R.J. Kaufmann, (New Jersey: Prentice-Hall, Inc., 1965), p. 74.
28. George Bernard Shaw, *Arms and the Man*, ed. A. C. Ward, (Hyderabad: Orient Longman, 1995), p. 2.
29. Margery M. Morgan, *The Shavian Playground: An Exploration of the Art of George Bernard Shaw*, (London: Methuen and Co. Ltd., 1972), p. 52.
30. *Arms and the Man*, pp. 2-3.
31. *Ibid*, p. 4.
32. C.B. Purdom, *A Guide to the Plays of Bernard Shaw*, p. 161.
33. *Arms and the Man*, p. 5
34. C.B. Purdom, *A Guide to the Plays of Bernard Shaw*, p. 157.
35. C.B. Purdom, *A Guide to the Plays of Bernard Shaw*, p.158.
36. *Ibid*, p. 58.
37. *Arms and the Man*, p. 51.
38. *Ibid*, p. 33.
39. *Ibid*, pp. 52-53.
40. *Ibid*, p. 53.
41. F. O' Donnel, "The Conflict of Wills in Shaw's Tragicomedy" in *G.B. Shaw: A Collection of Critical Essays*, ed. R.J. Kaufmann, (New Jersey: Prentice-Hall, Inc., 1965), p. 79.
42. Maurice Valency, *The Cart and the Trumpet: The Plays of George Bernard Shaw*, (New York: Oxford University Press, 1973), p. 111.

43. *Ibid*, pp. 111-112.
44. C.B. Purdom, *A Guide to the Plays of Bernard Shaw*, p. 247.
45. George Bernard Shaw, *Pygmalion*, ed. S. Sengupta, (Delhi: Surjeet Publications, 1985), p. 33.
46. *Ibid*, pp. 33-34.
47. C.B. Purdom, *A Guide to the Plays of Bernard Shaw*, p. 250.
48. *Pygmalion*, p. 142.
49. Louis Crompton, *Shaw the Dramatist: A Study of the Intellectual Background of The Major Plays*, (London: George Allen and Unwin Ltd., 1971), p. 147.
50. *Pygmalion*, p. 143.
51. *Ibid*, p. 115.
52. Louis Crompton, *Shaw the Dramatist: A Study of the Intellectual Background of The Major Plays*, pp. 146-147.
53. *Pygmalion*, p. 113.
54. Louis Crompton, *Shaw the Dramatist: A Study of the Intellectual Background of The Major Plays*, p. 147.
55. *Pygmalion*, p. 154.
56. *Ibid*, p. 153.
57. A.M. Gibbs, *The Art and Mind of Shaw: Essays in Criticism*, (London: The Macmillan Press Ltd., 1983), p. 170.
58. *Pygmalion* (Sequel), p. 124.
59. *Ibid*, p. 127.
60. A.M. Gibbs, *The Art and Mind of Shaw: Essays in Criticism*, p. 173.
61. *Pygmalion*, p. 110.
62. F. O' Donnel, "The Conflict of Wills in Shaw's Tragicomedy" in *G.B. Shaw: A Collection of Critical Essays*, ed. R.J. Kaufmann, p. 77.
63. C.B. Purdom, *A Guide to the Plays of Bernard Shaw*, p. 236.
64. George Bernard Shaw, *"Misalliance"*, in *Bernard Shaw: Complete Plays with Prefaces*, Vols. I to VI, (New York: Dodd, Mead & Company, 1962), p. 125. (Note: *Misalliance* is a rare play without any acts and scenes).
65. *Ibid*.
66. J.L. Wisenthal, *The Marriage of Contraries: Bernard Shaw's Middle Plays*, (Cambridge: Harvard University Press, 1974), p. 132.
67. *Ibid*, p. 142.
68. *Misalliance*, p. 65.

69. *Ibid*, p. 143.
70. *Misalliance*, p. 142.
71. *Ibid*, p. 163.
72. J.L. Wisenthal, *The Marriage of Contraries: Bernard Shaw's Middle Plays*, p. 129.
73. *Misalliance*, p. 162.
74. Michael Holroyd, *Bernard Shaw: The Pursuit of Power 1898-1918*, Vol. II, (London: Chatto and Windus, 1981), p. 249.
75. J.L. Wisenthal, *The Marriage of Contraries: Bernard Shaw's Middle Plays*, p, 129.
76. *Misalliance*, p. 164.
77. *Ibid*, p. 165.
78. *Ibid*, p. 177.
79. Maurice Valency, *The Cart and The Trumpet: The Plays of George Bernard Shaw*, (New York: Oxford University Press, 1973), p. 294.
80. *Misalliance*, p. 151.
81. C.B. Purdom, *A Guide to the Plays of Bernard Shaw*, pp. 195-196.
82. George Bernard Shaw, Prefatory Note, *"The Philanderer" in Bernard Shaw: Complete Plays with Prefaces*, Vols. I to VI, (New York: Dodd, Mead & Company, 1962), p. 724.
83. *Ibid*.
84. *The Philanderer*, p. 725.
85. Desmond MacCarthy, *SHAW*, p. 82.
86. C.B. Purdom, *A Guide to the Plays of Bernard Shaw*, p. 151.
87. *The Philanderer*, p. 733.
88. A.M. Gibbs, *The Art and Mind of Shaw: Essays in Criticism*, p. 63.
89. *Ibid*, p. 64.
90. *The Philanderer*, p. 790.
91. Margery M. Morgan, *The Shavian Playground: An Exploration of the Art of George Bernard Shaw*, p. 31.
92. *Ibid*, p. 34.
93. D.H. Laurence, ed., *Bernard Shaw: Collected Letters 1926-1950*, Vol. 4, p. 189.
94. *Ibid*, pp. 527-528.
95. Gareth Griffith, *Socialism and Superior Brains: The Political Thought of Bernard Shaw*, p. 167.

96. Desmond MacCarthy, *Shaw*, p. 79.

97. Gareth Griffith, *Socialism and Superior Brains: The Political Thought of Bernard Shaw*, p. 167.

98. A.M. Gibbs, *The Art and Mind of Shaw: Essays in Criticism*, p. 64.

99. *The Philanderer*, p. 781.

100. *Desmond MacCarthy, Shaw*, p. 82.

101. Margery M. Morgan, *The Shavian Playground: An Exploration of the Art of George Bernard Shaw*, p. 35.

3

Women in Profession

Economic independence is the keynote of Shavian Feminism. The stringent economic situation forces women to take up all sorts of job that consequently results in their exploitation. Shaw has portrayed the dilemma of professional women in a realistic way. For all the working women their work has supreme importance. Some of them smoke and drink also; all the relations that demand self-sacrifice are meagre and trivial to them. They have the ability and capacity to rise to any occasion. They confront the social conventions set for women and prove themselves to be self-made and self-driven. His professional women do not care much about societal concerns. They are physically well built and give strong handshakes; they can lift men on their shoulders and make them learn exercise. They study mathematics, business and participate in politics and family business; men run after them but uselessly. Shaw was very much impressed by all those women who took initiative in work and were proactive in their life. Contrary to general belief, his working partners had the beauty to launch a thousand ships. So his women characters are also charming and charismatic professionals, not worn out drudges. They are loved and admired for their eminence in life not for insignificance like a homely girl. This grit, right to self, makes them self-indulgent and is one of the aspects of the New Woman. Watson has encapsulated the Shavian professional woman:

> The Shavian career woman is many things nested in one, like a Russian wooden doll. Each of these stout painted women contains her smaller twin...[she] is an

> image of the great hidden potential of woman who is pregnant of...her grown-up self...[she] is criticism of society, is an embodiment of the divine spark, is a Bernard Shaw, is a dominant protective mother, is a virtual virgin to whom sex is given for safekeeping.[1]

Shaw's support of the working women is based on the good and welfare of society. *Mrs Warren in Mrs. Warren's Profession* exemplifies the catch-22 situation of the poor women. Vivie, in the same play, being an educated woman, stands against all the customary practises and opens the door for single women. Lina in *Misalliance* is a superwoman—adventurous, lifting boys and men, leading her life solely on her own terms, enjoying love-proposals. Louka, a maidservant not born to be a servant for her whole life, is a high flyer securing her own position by hook or by crook. All are intelligent and representative of different classes. Watson has written that "Shaw's career women work for a purpose larger than the self, just as his huntresses pursue fathers for their children, while the huntresses of other authors pursue husbands for themselves."[2] This grand purpose might be to raise self-conscience of women of different classes in the pecking order of society.

Vivie, in *Mrs. Warren's Profession*, is the best model of educated, professionally-trained, self-assertive woman, with the feeling of "individual independence," who vehemently asserts:

> People are always blaming their circumstances for what they are. I don't believe in circumstances. The people who get on in this world are the people who get up and look for the circumstances they want, and if they can't find them, make them.[3] (Act II)

She is the first unwomanly woman who emerges in Shavian drama: an unprecedented contrast to the conventional womanly woman of contemporary drama. On the suggestion of Beatrice Webb to create a play with a real, modern, unromantic, hard-working woman as a protagonist, Shaw paints Vivie as "an attractive specimen of the sensible, able, highly educated young middle class English woman."[4]

The play exhibits little sentiment and appeals more to conscience, chiefly the conscience of Vivie, who ultimately rejects the forces and compulsions of society for her own selfish ends (true presentation of "self" is what Shaw means by being selfish). Regarding the theme of conscience, *Mrs. Warren's Profession* may be called on expansion of the *Widowers' Houses*. Purdom, writing about it, comments:

> It is a hard play without sentiment, because conscience is hard, and Vivie's conscience is what the dramatic action is concerned with.... The personal problem is Vivie's with the background of the effects of capitalism, the position of women, morals, and social conscience.[5]

The stage directions describe Vivie as physically able-bodied, athletic and enthusiastic girl. She "shuts the gate with a vigorous slam" (Act I) and "brings the chair forward with one swing." (Act I) Her handshake numbs her mother's friend, Praed's fingers and the squeeze she gives to the robust Croft's hand makes him open his eyes and confess ruefully "she has a powerful fist." (Act I) Her relaxing recreation is mannish: when she gets tired she requires "a comfortable chair, a cigar, a little whisky and a novel with a good detective story." (Act I) She gets training of shooting with pistol from Frank and is a renowned mathematician, skilled in mathematical tripos at Cambridge and has tied with third Wranglar; Art, Music, opera she cannot withstand all these. All the characteristics are unwomanly making her an unwomanly woman figure. Vivie has never been portrayed as sentimental, fashionable and chic, unlike ordinary girls. Her ambition of life explicates the ambition of a real career woman. What is the Shavian ideology of a career woman? Answering this question Barbara Watson has written that the Shavian career woman is a melting pot who possesses her grown up self. This Shavian career woman is an incarnation of criticism of societal norms and assumptions about protective mother, virgin, womanly woman. Shaw has granted Vivie the right to a self as absolute as a man's. Her education, belief in conscience and her self-confidence in driving her own life on the less travelled path of being a single woman illustrate her right to a "self," uncommon in those days.

Having a business-oriented mind, Vivie has no interest in the wonderful world of art which Praed finds incredible to believe as he has never seen a woman without aesthetic sense. She is as much devoid of the sense of beauty and romance as her favourite subjects are mathematics and accounts. She discloses it herself "I would not go through that experience again for anything you could offer me. I held for civility's sake...I couldn't stand any more of it...." (Act I) Her pragmatic attitude predicts the incompatibility of her relationship with her mother in near future. She asserts, "Now you know the sort of perfectly splendid modern young lady I am. How do you think I shall get on with my mother?" (Act I) This is the result of her business sense that she has precognition of almost everything taking place in the course of the play. At the age of twenty-two she exhibits immense courage in all the things she does, startling those around her whether through her physical gestures and gesticulations or her explosive, outspoken, candid, matter-of-fact attitude even in the most sentimental situations. Whatever may come she remains unmoved and daring. She already assumes "I expect there will be a battle royal when my mother hears of my Chancery Lane projects." (Act I) She does not feel scared of the consequences of going against her mother's supposed "ideal" of being "little" Vivie.

"Hard as nails" and a "philistine" Vivie is unsentimental, so much so that she does not shrink from capitalizing on her mother also. She demands her right to know all the things about her mother with the "conventional superiority of a respectable woman." (Act II) For this demand of Vivie, Praed always warns Mrs. Warren to treat her as a grown woman and with every respect and to come out of the habit of thinking of her as a little girl. Crofts thinks that there's no resemblance between her and her mother. Frank's analysis of Vivie is also in the same rhapsodising way "Then you can have no idea what a girl she is, such character! Such sense! And her cleanness! Oh, my eye, Praed; but I can tell you she is clever!"[6] (Act I) This assessment of Vivie's character shows her bullish and discerning attitude towards her mother as well as others.

Vivie's relationship with her mother is a roller-coaster ride. For a long time she remains ignorant of her mother and her profession as well. She lives in a hostel and learns the way of life there. The characterisation of Vivie has a rise, fall and rise. She has a favourable impression of her mother in the very beginning; as the play progresses she depreciates her to penetrate the reality. After the revelation she sublimates her mother's status in her eye but by the end of the play she deserts her once and for all, giving both the women (herself and her mother) freedom of getting on with their destinies.

Vivie hates crying and tears and rebukes her mother, "Now pray don't begin to cry. Anything but that I really can't stand whimpering." (Act II) Her verbal duel with her mother is an optimum benchmark of her independent attitude:

> VIVIE. Then where are our relatives? My father? Our family friends? You claim the rights of a mother: the right to call me fool and child; to speak to me as no woman in authority over me at college dare speak to me; to dictate my way of life;...[7] (Act II)

The tension is evident between the mother and the daughter, between motherly tendency of possession and childish will of independence; but in fact this squabbling is what Vivie calls a struggle between "conventional authority of a mother" (Act II) and "conventional superiority of a respectable woman." (Act II) Here it should not be overlooked that both of them are professionals in their own respective fields and their differential socialisation makes them learn the lesson of overcoming problematic situation not to be overcome by it. Just after having such a deeply emotive and touching conversation, without the slightest feeling of sentiments, she speaks:

> VIVIE. Well that is enough for tonight. At what hour would you like breakfast? Is half past eight too early for you?
>
> MRS. WARREN [wildly] My God what sort of woman are you?
>
> VIVIE. [coolly] The sort the world is mostly made of, I should hope otherwise I don't understand how it gets its business done.[8] (Act II)

She behaves as if everything is of little value and makes no emotional appeal to her.

Vivie symbolises the traumatic effects of society inflicted on a woman. She reconciles with her mother's profession comprehending the worst situation on account of poverty and having no other alternative than to be good to some men. But Crofts, personifying capitalism, woos Vivie and being rejected, he turns the table. He apprises Vivie of the nasty continuance of the profession of her mother that comes to an end in her imagination. She cannot tolerate the stigma of living on the tainted money. This feeling that her upbringing depends on tainted money shakes the soul of conscience stricken Vivie and that in turn changes her conception of her mother. From "a wonderful woman...stronger than all England" (Act II) she turns into "the unmentionable woman [with] her capitalist bully." (Act III) Yet Vivie is found behaving sentimentally with her mother because for her condition she accuses the capitalist society. She admits before Crofts, "My mother was a poor woman who had no reasonable choice but to do as she did. You were a rich gentleman; and you did the same for the sake of 35 per cent. You are a pretty common sort of scoundrel...."[9] (Act III)

Vivie's refusal to the proposal of being Lady Crofts symbolises her denial of the capitalist society. Explaining the significance of her refusal Eric Bentley writes that Shaw does not show surrender to the system but [is] "intent on showing a rejection of the system. In the first instance, Vivie Warren's revolt represents Shaw's rational rejection of capitalism..."[10] Vivie abandons all the luxuries of life provided by her mother: this is significant as it depicts her stringent attack on capitalism.

Another aspect of Vivie's relationship is "love's young dream" (Act IV) which is shattered. The relationship of Vivie and Frank is not presented directly and fully. Frank is in love with Vivie, although she shows herself to be very unromantic, yet she loves him which is negated altogether as soon as she discovers the indirect and vague insinuation of their half brother and half sister relationship. We must remember that this is one of the gracious loves that are so uncharacteristic of Shaw. But Vivie knows from the very beginning the futility of "good for nothing" Frank. Before the disclosure of her incestuous romance she makes it clear to her mother, "I'm afraid so. Poor Frank! I shall have to get rid of him; but I shall feel sorry for him, though he's not worth it." (Act II) "The babes in the wood" Vivie and little Frank depart forever. Through this amalgamation of prostitution and incest Shaw wants to show the repercussions of it and his decision to leave it in lurch is to show the society an insoluble riddle engendered by society itself. Expressing the significance of Vivie-Frank relationship Eric Bentley writes, "Shaw combined the themes of prostitution and incest in order to make quite a rational point our mad society draws back in horror from [is] incest...it encourages prostitution, which is a virulent social pestilence."[11] He thus took an advanced position theoretically, just as Ibsen had done in *Ghosts*.

Vivie confronts the situations which try to lure her. Notwithstanding, she prefers to be a working bee, not a conventional romantic huntress in search of a prey. Her mother's profession, Frank's relation and Crofts' behaviour dishearten her severely yet she has the courage of living her life on her own conditions. She warns Praed and Frank:

> ...there are two subjects I want dropped, if you don't mind. One of them [to Frank] is love's young dream in any shape or form: the other [to Praed] is the romance and beauty of life.... If we three are to remain friends, I must be treated as a woman of business, permanently single [to Frank] and permanently unromantic [to Praed].[12] (Act IV)

The ultimate and absolute decision taken by Miss Warren is an unprecedented and historic resolution of a New Woman.

Vivie's decision of deserting her mother, despite her best endeavour and entreaties to regain her as a daughter, can be interpreted in various ways. No doubt, she looks a heartless daughter, devoid of all emotional attachment to her mother, but as a woman of conscience and business she takes the right step. She has been criticised for her hard-heartedness and as an unwomanly woman several times by several critics. Writing about Vivie a critic has observed, "The new woman of Shaw's conception is thus a degenerate hybrid with woman's body and man's mental and emotional toughness and is unfitted for her natural avocation."[13] Vivie hates crying, she knows that she cannot faint and cry; her "nasty" habit of smoking and her manly will power—all prove this idea true. For Shaw all these characteristics may prove to be the first step taken by woman to empower herself. Emphasising this point Gareth Griffith writes:

> ...in Shaw's view, the mimicking of male habits was an inevitable, if not welcome development in the struggle for emancipation from the mythology of the womanly woman. Even Vivie...perhaps the most sympathetic of the new women...takes up smoking...turns obsessively to work as a means of salvation; we are left at the close with a brave but rather lonely and shallow young woman who prefers the company of the abstractions found in account books to the complexities found in human character.[14]

She departs from her mother because of the incompatibility of their professions. She has a soft corner for her mother but both of them are professional women with their own professional ethics. Vivie is rather a step further from her mother since she is educated and single. Clarifying it she says:

> ...I am my mother's daughter. I am like you: I must have work, and must make more money than I spend. But my work is not your work, my way not your way. We must part. It will not make much difference to us: instead of meeting one another for perhaps a few months in twenty years, we shall never meet, that's all.[15] (Act IV)

Commenting on the secluded Vivie, Eric Bentley compares her to Saint Joan and writes "Vivie Warren is already a Saint Joan in that the experience Shaw gives her is that of being desolated."[16] Justifying Vivie for the final decision and Shaw's motive behind it, Martin L. Kornbluth in his article "Two Fallen Women: Paula Tanqueray and Kitty Warren," writes that Vivie represents the view of the playwright; she

> ...is never seriously disturbed by her mother's past.... Vivie's reasons for rejecting her mother are not moral ones—Kitty Warren, remaining what she was, simply did not fit into Vivie's life and her desire for a business career. Mrs. Warren is never really condemned for having done what she had; the nature of her work seems almost incidental to Vivie and to Shaw.... Shaw uses this particular sort of career, with all its sensational concomitants, merely to condemn the society which forces women into such ignoble means of earning a living.[17]

The Play *Misalliance* projects Lina Szczepanowska "the aviatrix-daredevil" whose proclamation may be considered as the keynote of Shavian Feminism:

> "I am an honest woman: I earn my living. I am a free woman: I live in my own house. I am a woman of the world," Lina declares, "...I am brave: I am independent: I am unbought: I am all that a woman ought to be..."[18]

Writing about the independent spirit of a womanly figure, Michael Holroyd says, "This solitary spirit was his [Shaw's] offering to feminism."[19] Lina's entrance is very significant as it is from the sky not from the earth; she lands in Tarleton's House in the garb of a man putting all in a fix and surprised about her identity. According to Michael Holroyd " Lina's appearance 'in full acrobatic trapeze dress, as dazzling as possible, to make her effect when she throws off her masculine cloak' is the most astonishing entrance to be made in a Shaw play."[20] After this the direction of the play changes. Earlier it is concerned about the words and thoughts but now it is subdued by action.

Lina is an adventurous Polish girl having all those characteristics which impart her the status of a New Woman. Her creation may have been startling and shocking when the play was staged in that period. She belongs to a family wherein it is customary for every member to put his or her life at stake, making it a point of honour. Lina is also doing the same for family reasons. Her sense of dressing up is quite manly. She says "I'm quite comfortable as I am. I am not accustomed to gowns: they hamper me and make me feel ridiculous."[21] Having listened to all her talks, all feel that they are dreaming about something. She adds a dreamlike element to their real, mundane capital-oriented and love-sick life. Shaw's purpose here is to show that dreams have more truth than reality. Actually the loopholes of aristocratic and capitalist class system which oppress not only women but all the human beings are attacked by Shaw. Observing it Michael Holroyd writes, "Shaw wants his audience to see that there is more truth in their dreams than in the actuality that has preceded it. The bomb he puts under the British class system is a comedy, and the fuse is his frustration."[22] According to Brecht Shaw is a terrorist who employs an unusual weapon of humour.[23]

Lina is a "singularly beautiful" woman who is very self confident and cocksure about her worth. Unlike other Victorian women, she has her own viewpoints and conception about herself and her future. During her conversation with Tarleton she gives voice to her cocky nature that makes them look aghast. She records the names of all those men who have proposed to her. But surprisingly she is never swayed by any of these proposals whether for the sake of money or love. The exaltation and adoration of her beauty and personality, almost by all the males, does not have any influence upon her. Tarleton's words in her praise "you touch chords. You appeal to the poetry in a man. You inspire him. Come now! You are a woman of the world: you're independent: you must have driven lots of men crazy..."[24] are not sufficient to negate her wildly independent spirit. She has a pragmatic and realistic approach to life and its ways. She tells Lord Summerhays about her spiritual conception of prayer to God, she redefines prayer and says that common people never pray to God. They always beg for something or the other. She prays to God for she has a soul. She does not beg for anything from God. Her self-complacency and self-fulfilment gives her a different stature from other common women who are always dissatisfied with whatsoever they have. Her calm and composed reaction to all the incidents make her sit on high pedestal. It is her profession to be "wonderful" and she is really "wonderful." We never get anything romantic from her side. Does it mean that she has no love and romance? Do independent women sacrifice love for the sake of freedom? Here she resembles Vivie Warren.

One thing very conspicuous about Lina is her slapping others and even lifting some of them on her shoulders. She "slaps" Tarleton "vigorously" and takes him by his arm to the gym to make him learn some exercises in order to teach how to stop crying. Lina lifts up Bentley also. We have to note the stage directions in this regard, "She [Lina] quickly lifts the upper half of Bentley from the ground; dives under him; rises with his body hanging across her shoulders; and runs out with him."[25] Lina has got virility quite opposite of Bentley who is endowed with womanly characteristics. Lina discovers a spiritual meaning in physical exercise and makes all the male members learn it in order to save their soul which is replete with love and romance only. In this way she has come from sky or heaven to work as a face-saver. Barbara Bellow Watson writes about her:

> This 'man-woman or woman-man whatever you call her' is unmistakably sent down from the skies (a dea ex machine whose airplane crashes into the green house) as a spiritual leader to the lost tribe of the underwear manufacturer.[26]

Lina acts as a "saving woman" who saves the aristocratic family of Bentley, capitalists family of Mr. Tarleton. She reveals that there is something more in life than only marriage proposals and lovemaking. Barbara Watson further adds, "Lina...is ...a saving woman...not in the direct line—Lady to Major to Saint-in the sense of being a public personage. All her saving is done in one idle sick household, a foretaste of *Heartbreak House*."[27] Lina is real and pragmatic and her grit to face reality comes of her profession of acrobat wherein she faces death and responsibility together. She explains that on the flying trapeze there are two or more women whose lives are in each other's hands. She risks her life once a day as a "point of honor" prays for her own soul and considers marriage as a "degrading slavery." She demonstrates the vigour, vitality and unconventionality which are certainly worth of being a saint.[28]

Shaw has modelled Lina to some extent on Aurêlie in *Love Among the Artists* for which he got inspiration from Marie Bashkirtseff, but there is a subtle difference. Watson alludes to this hidden point:

> Shaw created the counterpart of Aurélie a quarter of a century late in Misalliance, Lina Szczepanowska is an acrobat who has more in common with Aurêlie than just a name which Englishman pride themselves on being enable to pronounce. She too is modelled to some extent on Marie Bashkirtseff, but Shaw makes one subtle adaptation. By making his characters Polish instead of Russian, he invokes the spirit of Chopin and Mickiewicz, of art and the spirit of romantic revolutionary nationalism, and also an incisiveness, a medieval European iron which is not believed to characterise the

> Russian ambience. Lina, the later creation, has all these qualities to an even greater degree than her predecessor. Her career as an acrobat calls even more sharply for discipline, for self making, for rising above the mere woman, than do even the demands of fine art.[29]

Lina is a harbinger of true emancipation and freedom for women. Lina's denunciation, near the end of the play, on the stereotyped role of women and their socialization to conform to it, is very relevant in the light of women related issues. She says:

> You seem to think of nothing but making love.... Your women are kept idle and dressed up for no other purpose than to be made love to. I have not been here an hour; and already everybody makes love to me as if because I am a woman it were my profession to be made love to....[30]

She raises the question of being an object of love and sex. Can any woman go beyond it? Can she take decision about her own life? In this regard she shows some glimpses of Vivie Warren who goes beyond the human charms of love and marriage. Through her bold speech on the lovemaking as central and pervasive influence or motive in the family, Lina makes the world think of the wastage of energy. J.L. Wisenthal writes that *Misalliance* and *Heartbreak House* have similarities as in:

> ...both plays we have the sense of strong energies that cannot find any satisfying expression, and which therefore run to talk and to sexual pursuit...[Lina's] speech is valid as a comment on the waste of energy in the world of the play.[31]

Most of the characters seem to run after something or the other and live "unfulfilled lives" with the notable exception of the outsiders Lina and Percival.

The balance of mental, physical and emotional faculties of Lina requires the balance of masculine and feminine (not in the eye of Shaw) characteristics. Lina is a "mongrel" as she:

> ...combines feminine attractiveness with masculine bravery and strength, a union which is reflected in Hypatia's definition of her as 'the man-woman or

> woman-man....' This combination, in Lina, of physical and spiritual superiority and male female qualities, is an anticipation of Saint Joan.[32]

Thus she has androgynous personality. Lina's character is paradoxical as she combines those male and female traits which Shaw ridiculed in *Arms and the Man*: "Coolness in the face of physical danger and fealty to abstract honor," and the androgynous point of view proves its value here. A woman saying "you can't cover me with the pistol." Try is not just a "novelty" but a realignment of moral forces. Shaw is doing new thing by transposing old values into a new gender. Thus Shaw combines in her legendary masculine traits of being cool, composed, calm and adventurous.[33] This perfection in Lina, Valency says is "an example of the superwoman" and "exceptionally touchy woman" who is revolted by the idea of marriage than the idea of love. Lina's alliance with Bentley might serve the undeclared purpose of Life Force. Valency is of the view that through Lina Shaw may be trying to project some biological operation of the Life Force. However his purpose at this stage remains not very apparent and explicit.[34]

Louka in *Arms and the Man* is representative of all those workingwomen who are aware of the society they live in and its ways. They know their wishes, aspirations and how to activate those desires. Through the character of Louka, Shaw has portrayed professional women, competent and conscious enough to turn the situation in their favour and take everything in their stride. She does not exemplify the victimised workingwomen who put their life, dignity at stake. The following dialogue exemplifies her dauntless courage:

> Look at me! How much am I allowed to have my own will? I have to get your room ready for you: to sweep and dust, to fetch and carry. How could that degrade me if it did not degrade you to have it done for you? If I were Empress of Russia, above everyone in the world, then!!... I would marry the man I loved which no other queen in Europe has the courage to do....[35] (Act III)

Louka knows how to raise her social standards. In spite of being a maidservant she does not possess a servant's soul. She scolds Nicola, "yes: sell your manhood for 30 levas, and buy me for 10! (Rising scornfully) keep your money. You were born to be a servant. I was not." (Act III) She is an ambitious, shrewd and unscrupulous girl, who tries to get success by all means. Her conversation with Nicola, time and again, reflects that she is a social climber. She threatens Nicola, "You'll never put the soul of a servant into me." (Act II) Undoubtedly, her conduct, her gait, her presence of mind, her trickery shows the least of a servant's conforming attitude. She smokes "cigaret." (Act II) She has the spirit of a defiant social rebel. Her pent up feelings are explosive which turn the whole action of the play.

Act II belongs to Louka, her attitude, thoughts, aspirations, her innermost feelings get reflection in this act. She proclaims without any fear of getting sacked that she disobeys Raina and her mother Catherine—Louka's mistresses. She says, "I do defy her. I will defy her. What do I care for." (Act II) She even prepares the ground for her protection as she knows the family secrets. She is basically an eavesdropper who makes use of her master's secrets that we later observe in her conversation with Sergius. She reveals to Sergius that Raina would marry the "chocolate cream soldier" although she does not know his name. It is this unscrupulous bent of mind which compels Sergius, in a manipulative manner, to accept Louka as his soul mate.

Louka is witty as well as pretty. Just as Bluntschilli foils the utopian higher love of Raina, in the same way Louka shatters Sergius's dream of true, immaculate love. She is strong-willed and ensnares Sergius, taking benefit of his philandering nature. Sergius makes love to her behind Raina's back and she gets the chance to poison his ear against Raina. In fact, she speaks the truth. She says "I don't want your kisses, gentle folk are all alike: you making love to me behind Miss Raina's back; and she doing the same behind yours." (Act II) She comments on Sergius's hypocrisy and calls him a coward.

Louka foretells that Raina would marry Bluntschilli if he comes to her again. Her forethought is absolutely true. She also explains that the behaviour of Sergius and Raina with each other is a mere show off and not real. She says to Sergius:

> ...I tell you that if that gentleman ever comes here again, Miss Raina will marry him, whether he likes it or not. I know the difference between the sort of manner you and she put on before one another and the real manner.[36] (Act II)

Louka observes the conduct very vigilantly and reveals it daringly. She is not at all afraid of her own criticism rather she weighs her own self and compares herself to Raina proclaiming her own superiority. She says:

> ...you know how to hurt with your tongue as well as with your hands. But I don't care, now I've found out that whatever clay I'm made of, you're made of the same. As for her, she's a liar; and her fine airs are a cheat; and I'm worth six of her (She shakes the pain off hardily; tosses her head; and sets to work to put the things on the tray).[37] (Act II)

Instead of crying and weeping she shakes her pain off and regards her work just like a true professional, unlike womanly woman shedding tears over accusation and nasty remarks, she throws it back and retaliates confidently which shows the complacency of a business-like woman.

Louka capitalises on "the apostle of the higher love" Sergius's flippant, chicken-hearted, weak, hypocritical attitude. She makes him realize that he can be brave if he dares to propose Louka. She says "I wonder are you really a brave man?... How easy it is to talk! Men never seem to me to grow up: they all have schoolboy's ideas. You don't know what true courage is." (Act III) She threatens him that if Raina marries the Swiss, Sergius would come back to Louka and she would reject him. She drags Sergius into catch-22 situation and speaks "A man [The Swiss] worth ten of you. Then you can come to me; and I will refuse you. You are not good enough for me." (Act III) She reads Sergius's nerves and acts accordingly. She compares him with Bluntschilli and shatters his personal belief of superiority, snobbery and treats him psychologically and makes him marry her and do what she wants.

The relationship between Louka and Raina is always without words. They hardly talk to each other except about some household chores. Louka just flies a kite to get the feel of Raina's inner most feelings towards Bluntschilli:

> LOUKA. (knowing instinctively that she can annoy Raina by disparaging Bluntschilli). He has not much heart, that Swiss. He has not a word of grief for his poor father.
>
> RAINA. (bitterly) Grief! A man who has been doing nothing but killing people for years! What does he care? What does any soldier care? (She goes to door, restraining her tears with difficulty).[38] (Act III)

Louka is searching Raina's heart to know her deep feelings about him and she is successful in her pursuit that her prior judgement is somewhat true. At the end of the play Louka is caught red-handed listening to all the things standing behind the door. She is not shameful of eavesdropping as she says, "my love was at stake. I am not ashamed.... My love, stronger than anything you [Raina] can feel...." (Act III) At last she is successful in her strategy of getting Sergius as her husband.

During the course of the play Louka has been addressed as "abominable little clod of common clay," (Act III) "Viper" having "a soul above her station." One who sets her own "fashion" and at last victorious Louka proves Shaw's belief in being "unashamed" to fulfil one's desire. Shaw never believed in the ideal of womanly woman. He always repudiates the self-sacrificing nature of woman. In that way Louka is not like a "female conformer to the ideal of womanliness." In *The Womanly Woman* Shaw writes, "... a womanly woman is not only taken advantage of, but disliked as well for her pains."[39] Thus Louka is a modern woman who climbs the social ladder by virtue of her own strong will, strategy and implementation. She does not rave for her love, she wins it, thwarting whole "basketful of ideals" concerned with womanly woman. She may be labelled as a femme fatale, selfish, opportunist, unwomanly, manly etc., but if a man had behaved in like manner he would have been exalted for it. If a woman adopts the less-travelled path she is criticised for it. Louka walks on this path and remains victorious. She fulfils what she wants. This is called real equality of man and woman. The later workingwomen in *The Millionairess*, and in other plays, have the same traits of Louka. Louka is the embryo of other career women who are full-fledged, grown up, matured example of this little seed.

Shaw is absolutely right when he categorically states that *Mrs. Warren's Profession* belongs to all those victimised women trapped in the crude clutches of society yet society pays no heed to their lot evolved by the shoddy conditions of society itself. He wrote:

> I simply affirm that *Mrs. Warren's Profession* is a play for women; that it was written for women; that it has been performed and produced mainly through the determination of women that it should be performed and produced; that the enthusiasm of women made its first performance excitingly successful; and that not one of these women had any inducement to support it except their belief in the timeliness and the power of the lesson the play teaches.[40]

Mrs. Warren, the central figure of the play, is a society made courtesan not a self-made whore. She represents all those innocent victims who have no other alternative but to adopt prostitution as a source of livelihood to survive in a society which cannot provide two daily meals to them. Shaw has avoided displaying the common notion of hatred towards prostitutes: on the other hand he sides with them. In the preface to *Mrs. Warren's Profession* he says:

> Prostitution is caused, not by female depravity and male licentiousness, but simply by underpaying, undervaluing, and overworking women so shamefully that the poorest of them are forced to resort to prostitution to keep body and soul together.[41]

Through the character of Mrs. Warren, Shaw has accused the society for not providing respectable, honourable, women-friendly careers. Mrs. Warren is one of the many "fallen" women in literature [who were punished by society in different ways]. She is an affluent boss of a syndicate that organises and manages international brothels under the garb of hotels. She is initiated into this profession of prostitution, as there is no other option left for her to survive in the world. She explains to Vivie the abominable, squalid condition of factories and other working places; and the scornful way in which she is treated by her masters and customers; discerning that all the other professions for women are blind alleys she turns around in a new direction towards prostitution. Commenting on her situation Purdom says:

> She herself had taken to the prostitute's career because there was no other escape from life of grinding poverty. Having a head for business and a sister who had a head for business, too, she capitalised her good looks, and was so successful that she got financial support to operate on a large scale.[42]

It is an irony that when she wishes to do respectable work she finds no supportive hands to help and encourage her.

Mrs. Warren, a woman between 40 and 50, was "formerly pretty, showily dressed in a brilliant hat and a gay blouse fitting tightly over her bust and flanked by fashionable sleeves. Rather spoilt and domineering, and decidedly vulgar, but, on the whole, genial and fairly presentable," (Act I) she is one of Shaw's career women. Though a degraded prostitute Mrs. Warren shares one of the prominent features of Shavian woman that she remains to be a saving mother, a protective figure. She epitomizes "the Virgin Mother." Elaborating the concept of Virgin Mother apart from Christianity, Margery M. Morgan writes, "The Virgin Mother is featured...as a protective figure, inhibiting to crude masculinity, and antithetically balanced against the 'novel and bold moral attitude,' the 'self-respect' of the actress."[43] Mrs. Warren exhibits the same sense of protection and authority over her daughter, Vivie, and accept even the role of the father. Crofts says of her "I have asked her (about Vivie's father), often enough. But she's so determined to keep the child all to herself that she would deny that it ever had a father if she could."[44] (Act I) It shows Shaw's mother fixation and his belief in mother-dominated families endemic in most of his plays which emanates from his autobiographical knowledge. Mrs. Warren is such a concerned mother that she remains blind to her growing, and independent minded daughter. She has much of the business acumen which gets reflected in her conversation with Frank regarding his relationship with Vivie. Her clear cut, outspoken, commercial way of handling human relations is really creditable. She scolds Frank and lets him down: "Your love's a pretty cheap commodity, my lad. If you have no means of keeping a wife, that settles it: you can't have Vivie." (Act II) She is similarly reprimanded at the end of the play when Vivie asserts her resolution: "It's no use, mother: I am not to be changed by a few cheap tears and entreaties any more than you are, I daresay."[45] (Act IV)

Compared to other characters, Mrs. Warren has lots of complexities. Since she is a professional woman, and mother also, she responds to the various demanding personalities in suitable ways. As a skilled, experienced businesswoman she deals with Frank, Praed and Crofts with cavalier attitude and scathing rebuke; her experienced mind's eye discerns the motive of Crofts and reproaches him for his ill will. Mrs. Warren warns Crofts "What are you up to about that girl? I've been watching your way of looking at her. Remember: I know you and what your looks mean.... I would put you out and pack you back to London pretty soon if I saw any of your nonsense. My girl's little finger is more to me than your body and soul."[46] (Act II)

Mrs. Warren explains to Vivie the squalid condition of factories and other working places where the working conditions are so disastrous that it can make any living being dead flesh. She says that she has not been brought up like Vivie who has had the best education without getting a glimpse of poverty. She talks about the miserable conditions of her two half sisters who were

> ...undersized, ugly, starved-looking, hard working, honest poor creatures...what did they get by their respectability? One of them worked in a white lead factory twelve hours a day for nine shillings a week until she died of lead poisoning.... The other...married a Government labourer... and kept his room and the three children neat and tidy on eighteen shillings a week—until he took to drink. That was worth being respectable for, wasn't it?[47] (Act II)

She justifies what she is as she does not want to be poor because poverty induces a person to do anything in order to get money. She asserts:

> ...if there's a thing I hate in a woman, it's want of character...of course it's [profession of a prostitute] worthwhile to a poor girl...and a girl must make the best of it. But of course it's not worthwhile for a lady. If you took to it you'd be a fool; but I should have been a fool I'd taken to anything else."[48] (Act II)

The question of having self-respect does not arise when a girl is living in starvation and slavery. Mrs. Warren is an independent woman and is able to give her daughter good education because she is making money as much as she wants by any means. Her philosophy in life being "The only way for a woman to provide for herself decently is for her to be good to some man that can afford to be good to her" (Act II) whether by marriage or by prostitution. To some extent, Shaw is right in making this bold statement but his outlook has been criticised and has drawn fire by critics. Germaine Greer thinks that Shaw concentrates upon brothel keepers and formulates his conception of working woman.

> Germaine Greer [writes] in concentrating on the affairs of a wealthy madam of a continental brothel the play ignored all but the tiniest minority of successful prostitutes; 'Shaw's argument seems to be that all working-class girls are whores who can be. The rest are the plain losers.[49]

Mrs. Warren's Profession is thus a definite and strong portrayal of the economic independence of women. Mrs. Warren's relationship with Frank is a temporary phase and at times she feels tempted and kisses him; but the next moment she fathoms the gravity and urgency of her relation and the situation as well and it makes her flinch. Her relationship with her daughter has different phases. At the beginning of the play when Vivie was ignorant of her mother's profession, she is portrayed as a very dependent, squeamish, innocent schoolchild. As time passes Mrs. Warren realizes that she is not only her daughter but a fully mature, grown up, sensible woman of twenty-one who very well knows her rights and prerogatives. The conversation between Mrs. Warren and her daughter reveals a conventional maternal aspect of a prosperous professional woman as well as a victim of society.

Shaw does not portray even a prostitute as a "fiend" and termagant rather he supports her indirectly by delineating the other side of her as well in a very positive manner. It does not mean that Shaw approves of her profession for any woman; but neither does he blame woman for her wretched condition that makes her bring about her own destruction. In an article "Two Fallen Women, Paula Tanqueray and Kitty Warren," Martin L. Kornbluth writes:

> Instead of attempting to apologize and entreat forgiveness and begin a new life Kitty Warren puts her accusers on the defensive, justifying completely in the audience's mind her conduct. She too wants a reconciliation with her daughter, but not at the expense of sacrificing the handsome income she still gets from her profession.[50]

Mrs. Warren does not commit suicide like Pinero's Paula Tanqueray, she does not give up her profession either nor does she repents for her condition. She accuses the whole society and justifies her self-respect and her financial status. "The life suits me: I'm fit for it and not for anything else.... No: it's no use; I can't give it up—not for anybody." (Act IV) These words show that she is not remorseful for her earlier indiscretions. Thus Shaw does not make her bow to the conventional morality of the society.

Initially after the revelation of her mother's profession Vivie is not very much disturbed and takes it casually and displays very congenial feelings for her mother; she never condemns her mother. What is unbearable is her mother's denial to abandon her profession forever. Commenting on Mrs. Warren's will and wish to continue her profession of the so-called hotel business, Bernard F. Dukore in his article "The Fabian and the Freudian" writes that whatever profession an individual chooses is a reflection of the personality of the individual. Mrs. Warren resumes her profession despite being rich. Her sister Liz quits the same profession as soon as she gets the chance. What Bernard F. Dukore figures out from Dr. Greewald's study on prostitutes that apart from economic needs there are certain emotional experiences which mould a call girl's personality leading her to continue the profession. Shaw examines not only the social causes which lead to prostitution but also the psychological factors which make a woman continue with the profession. The reasons behind Mrs. Warren's compulsions are social as well as psychological. Her last words "the life suits me: I'm fit for it and not for anything else" can be taken to support many psychological factors. Thus the orientation of this drama becomes more sociological and psychological, but the psychology is not deliberated or analysed.

Despotic and dictatorial Shavian woman combats the oppressive society face to face; yet unlike other canonical female protagonists, she remains un-crucified and un-penalized. Although Mrs. Warren is somewhat punished by nature and society, she is not ashamed of her profession nor is she conscience-stricken and humiliated. She says, "If people arrange the world that way for women there is no good pretending it's arranged the other way—No I never was a bit ashamed really."[51] (Act II) She imposes the liability of her misfortune on socio-economic trends carried by the society and remains "unashamed." Barbara Watson discusses this diffused element of being "unashamed" in all Shavian heroes and heroines; she says "Shaw does not punish Mrs. Warren in *Mrs. Warren's Profession*...he does not grind his heroine down according to the flamboyant terms of what Kenneth Tyhan calls 'the dramatist's convention'."[52]

> ...in Mrs. Warren's Profession Shaw had outraged public opinion by showing a successful prostitute who lived by that motto.... Shaw gifts his strong characters with an awareness that the guilt is society's for having offered them two evils as alternatives, not theirs for having chosen the lesser.[53]

Mrs. Warren epitomises the true and genuine portrayal of economic misfortune. Basically the play and its central figure, Mrs. Warren, is a reminder of one of the world's most resolutely ignored facts; that is the sexual exploitation of women who are not prostitutes. Mrs. Warren succumbs to this exploitation of society because she does not have university education; when Vivie is exploited in the same way by Crofts and Frank she, being an educated woman, struggles and protects herself. Shaw's women are a part of larger social issues, Mrs. Warren is also a part of a big social framework of prostitution. Shaw's support of the workingwomen is based on his aim for improvement of the whole society. Mrs. Warren's last words show the mental agony and trauma of a "survivor," not a victim, as Shaw intends to project her:

> I always wanted to be a good woman. I tried honest work; and I was slave driven until I cursed the day I ever heard of honest work. I was a good mother; and because I made my daughter a good woman she turns me out as if I was a leper. Oh, if I only had my life to live over again! ...I'd do wrong and nothing but wrong and I'll prosper on it."[54]

She continues to do "wrong" in the world's eye not in Shaw's and her own.

Shaw's women in profession are involved in their work only for two reasons: to get money and to be successful. By their eminence and achievement they prove that high accomplishment and professionalism are almost inextricable and indistinguishable. These women exchange the fripperies of feminity for the armor of feminism. They have got "right to self" absolutely free to rise high, without paying heed to social limitations. Shaw's working women are not stay-at-home writers and actresses rather they are acrobats, mathematicians, social achievers and remorseless heads. Shaw does not prefer a secretary, a research assistant, a dietician as his characters because these designations represent a new kind of female subjugation. His successful women have strong "will" which strengthens their soul to get what they want. They are represented as bosses fit to rule, rather than as subordinates to be ruled.

REFERENCES

1. Barbara Bellow Watson, *A Shavian Guide to the Intelligent Woman*, (London: Chatto and Windus, 1964), p. 149.

2. *Ibid*, p. 151.

3. George Bernard Shaw, *Mrs. Warren's Profession in Bernard Shaw: Complete Plays with Prefaces*, vols. I-VI, (New York: Dodd, Mead & Company, 1962), p. 65.

4. Sonja Lorichs, "The Unwomanly Woman." *The Shavian* 7th 8th Ser. 4 (Summer, 1973), pp. 250-254.

5. C.B. Purdom, *A Guide to the Plays of Bernard Shaw*, (Methuen: London University Paperbacks, 1963), p. 155.
6. *Mrs. Warren's Profession*, p. 46.
7. *Ibid*, p. 63.
8. *Ibid*, p. 64.
9. *Ibid*, p. 83.
10. Eric Bentley, "The Making of a Dramatist (1892-1903)" in *G.B. Shaw: A Collection of Critical Essays*, ed. R.J. Kaufmann, (New Jersey: Prentice-Hall, Inc., 1965), p. 72.
11. *Ibid*, p. 73.
12. *Mrs. Warren's Profession*, p. 93.
13. Savitri Khanna, "Shaw's Image of Woman", *The Shavian* 7th 8th Ser. 4 (Summer, 1973), pp. 253-259.
14. Gareth Griffith, *Socialism and Superior Brains: The Political Thought of Bernard Shaw*, (London: Rougledge, 1993), p. 168.
15. *Mrs. Warren's Profession*, p. 102.
16. Eric Bentley, "The Making of a Dramatist (1892-1903)" in *G.B. Shaw: A Collection of Critical Essays*, p. 72.
17. Martin L. Kornbluth, "Two Fallen Women: Paula Tanqueray and Kitty Warren" *The Shavian*, Ser. 14, (Feb. 1959), pp. 14-15.
18. George Bernard Shaw, *Misalliance in Bernard Shaw: Complete Plays with Prefaces*, vols. I-VI, (New York: Dodd, Mead & Company, 1962), p. 201. (Note: Misalliance is a rare play without any acts and scenes).
19. Michael Holroyd, *Bernard Shaw: The Pursuit of Power, 1898-1918*, Vol. II, (London: Chatto and Windus, 1989), p. 249.
20. *Ibid*, p. 247.
21. *Misalliance*, p. 154.
22. Michael Holroyd, *Bernard Shaw: The Pursuit of Power, 1898-1918*, Vol. II, p. 247.
23. *Ibid*.
24. *Misalliance*, p. 159.
25. *Ibid*, pp. 187-188.
26. Barbara Bellow Watson, *A Shavian Guide to the Intelligent Woman*, p. 168.
27. *Ibid*.
28. *Ibid*.
29. *Ibid*, p. 160.

30. *Misalliance*, p. 200.
31. J.L. Wisenthal, *The Marriage of Contraries: Bernard Shaw's Middle Plays*, (Cambridge: Harvard University Press, 1974), p. 128.
32. *Ibid*, p. 134.
33. Barbara Bellow Watson, *A Shavian Guide to the Intelligent Woman*, p. 160.
34. Maurice Valency, *The Cart and The Trumpet: The Plays of George Benard Shaw*, (New York: OUP, 1973), p. 224.
35. George Bernard Shaw, *Arms and the Man*, ed. A.C. Ward, (Hyderabad: Orient Longman, 1995), p. 60.
36. *Ibid*, p. 36.
37. *Ibid*, pp. 36-37.
38. *Ibid*, p. 56.
39. George Bernard Shaw, *The Quintessence of Ibsenism* (London: Constable & Co., 1913), p. 32.
40. *Mrs. Warren's Profession*, Preface, p. 21.
41. *Ibid*, p. 3.
42. C.B. Purdom, *A Guide to the Plays of Bernard Shaw*, p. 154.
43. Margery M. Morgan, *The Shavian Playground: An Exploration of the Art of George Bernard Shaw*, (London: Methuen and Co. Ltd., 1972), p. 74.
44. *Mrs. Warren Profession*, p. 44.
45. *Ibid*, p. 103.
46. *Ibid*, p. 58.
47. *Ibid*, pp. 65-66.
48. *Ibid*, p. 68.
49. Gareth Griffith, *Socialism and Superior Brains: The Political Thought of Bernard Shaw*, p. 114.
50. Martin L. Kornbluth, "Two Fallen Women: Paula Tanqueray and Kitty Warren" *The Shavian*, pp. 14-15.
51. *Mrs. Warren Profession*, p. 70.
52. Barbara Bellow Watson, *A Shavian Guide to the Intelligent Woman*, p. 20.
53. *Ibid*.
54. *Mrs. Warren Profession*, p. 104.

4

Women as Driving Force

Shaw always reposed his strong faith in the saving goodness of women. His optimistic views about women as saviours are personified in this category; some of the women Shaw has portrayed as driving force. As Watson has written, "The author, though himself a professional talk maker, does not believe that the world can be saved by talk alone...his own favourite is the woman of action...."[1] Driving Force is a modernised form of nineteenth century traditional saving women who were characterised as "prig...artificially constructed without selfishness, without animal instincts, without the weakness of common humanity."[2] Shaw has asserted the strength of these weaknesses as "The twentieth century saving woman is called upon to save society, to save the world."[3] They not only drive themselves but also their family, society and world. Besides being housekeepers, homemakers and daughters they exercise authority and control over others. They take men as their children, to be taught values and importance of women. Like professional women, they also confront the society but not only for themselves but also for their family and society as well. They are more universal than women in love and women in profession as both the categories present only two extremes—absolute acceptance of love, and absolute negation of love. But women in this category do not opt for lopsided life but for evenly balanced life. They are working women as well as agents of Life Force. They have the moral attributes of devotion and self sacrifice for the common good of the society. Major Barbara, Lady Britomart, Candida, Grace represent different sides of saving women. Major Barbara, in spite of lack of money tries to save the soul of people. Lady Britomart presents a saving mother. Candida saves the dignity of invisible homemaker and Grace protects the (future) women from falling prey to the traps of men. The difference between women as driving force and true professionals is that the former are working for a purpose of saving something or the other; but working bees work for themselves, for their survival not for society.

While motherhood has been a great source of women's oppression Bernard Shaw explores and finds out that this is the area in which women have typically exercised power through their control and authority over other human beings. Candida is one of the powerful, emancipated mothers created by Shaw. As Morgan has written:

> ...the conventionality of *Candida* is more striking than the 'revolt' it contains...[it] presents a view antithetical to that of Ibsen's *Doll's House*: instead of woman as the immature play thing of man, Shaw emphasizes her maternal aspect, her influence over men and their dependence on her strength.[4]

Candida is identified first as a mother who mothers grown up men; she is the driving force of her husband Morell and visitor Eugene. Regarding her role Shaw wrote to William Archer, "Candida...is a mother first, a wife twenty seventh, and nothing else."[5] She has the potential of drive(ing) anyone out of their senses. Stage directions describe her as a mother of two children who do not appear during the course of the play. When Candida enters the scene of action, she is introduced as "looking at them (Morell and Burgess) with an amused maternal indulgence which is her characteristic expression." (Act I) She is a woman with the double charm of youth and motherhood. Candida mothers two grown up babies Morell and Eugene Marchbanks with the labor of her hands and the love of her heart. She is the entirety of all loving care to them—wife, mother and sisters.

At the beginning of the play, Candida is introduced to readers and audiences by word of mouth, Morell suggests Lexy to fall ill and be nursed by Candida. Morell considers his married life a replica of the kingdom of heaven. He suggests Lexy to get a wife like Candida. Morell's continuous appreciation of his wife makes Prossy irritable. She complains, "Candida here, and Candida there, and Candida everywhere! It's enough...to hear a woman raved about in that absurd manner." (Act I) But later on she also feels compelled to praise her. Candida always addresses Marchbanks and Morell as a "poor boy," a "dear boy," "very nice boy" and a "great baby," a "bad boy." Thus Shaw wants to put emphasis on the maternal aspect of Candida and this is the reason her children never come on the stage. Gail Finney writes, "By keeping her two actual children off in the country throughout the play, however, Shaw foregrounds her mothering of adults."[6] The childlike status of Marchbanks and Morell vis-à-vis Candida is crystal clear when Morell sits in children's chair and Marchbanks sits in visitor's chair in Act III. This symbolises the infantilization of grown ups by Candida. Bernard Shaw's every woman almost addresses her husband or fiancé or lover as baby and shows a mother-like caring attitude. In this regard Candida resembles the baby-talking Vivie Warren in *Mrs. Warren's Profession* and Barbara in *Major Barbara* who calls her fiancé as her "dear little Dolly boy." All these female figures manifest that motherly tendency which is very necessary in a compatible husband wife relationship. Freud considers this mothering of a husband or a lover by wife very important for conjugal bliss as he writes in "Feminity":

> A mother is only brought unlimited satisfaction by her relation to a son; this altogether the most perfect, the most free from ambivalence of all human relationships.... Even a marriage is not made secure until the wife has succeeded in making her husband her child as well and in acting as a mother to him.[7]

As a mother figure Candida is identified with the Virgin Mary—an embodiment of ideal motherhood. Shaw describes Candida as "the poetry of the wife and mother—the Virgin mother in the true sense."[8] Through the stage directions Candida's affinity with Virgin Mary is also expressed. As Candida enters the play for the first time Shaw's directions specify her as:

> A wise hearted observer, looking at her [Candida], would at once guess that whoever had placed the Virgin of the Assumption over her hearth did so because he fancied some spiritual resemblance between them..."[9] (Act I)

As virgin mother Candida mothers everyone; Eugene Marchbanks says to her that taking her name is a "prayer" to him, a formation of happiness, "heaven," and the moments spent with her give him a sense of the "silent glory of life." Whenever Eugene; is attacked by Morell and Burgess Candida comes to "the rescue" of Eugene but when Morell is disturbed and nagged by Eugene and gets into furious tizzy, Candida protects him also, calling him a "boy." Marchbanks's description to Morell about Candida's offering is highly evocative of the Virgin. She offers "her shawl, her wings, the wreath of stars on her head, the lilies in her hand, the crescent moon beneath her feet." (Act III) He has the vision of Candida not with a scrubbing brush, but in a boat: "a tiny shallop to sail away in, far from the world, where the marble floors are washed by the rain and dried by the sun; where the south wind dusts.... Or a chariot! to carry us up into the sky, where the lamps are stars...."[10] (Act II) Thus Marchbanks's fantasy and the myth of the Virgin of Assumption are clear. It seems that Marchbanks wants to be inspired by a desire to refuse the physicality of Candida. By giving Candida a Godlike status Shaw has his own purpose. Margery M. Morgan writes:

> By linking the sway of the central female figure with a sacred Christian image on the one hand and, on the other, with associations outside the Christian tradition, the dramatist has transformed a private symbol into an emblem of a whole society and the psychological pattern which he sees determining its character.[11]

Shaw has sublimated a common, down-to-earth woman to the status of Virgin Mother in order to uplift the role of mother because mother's role is often reduced to nonentity. Candida symbolises all those mute, silent fulltime homemakers who exercise authority over their family members. Thus Shaw has turned the table in favour of a woman.

Candida is loved and respected by Eugene as well as by Morell but in different ways. Both of them claim to understand Candida. Both the male characters are professional men of words, a preacher and a poet. Marchbanks charges Morell that he is a moralist and "windbag" who does not understand the real value of Candida, her soul which craves for something higher. Marchbanks tells Morell that Candida hates his preaching. To some extent he is right because later Candida speaks frankly:

> Ah, James, how little, you understand me, to talk of your confidence in my goodness and purity! I would give them both to poor Eugene as willingly as I would give my shawl to a beggar dying of cold, if there were nothing else to restrain me.[12]

Candida pays no heed to the Victorian values like "purity" and "goodness" associated with women and for her they do not hold any significance; rather she makes Morell feel that they are as trivial as a shawl. She breaks all the norms set by the society only for women. Marchbanks is right in his assessment of Candida's viewpoint about Morell's preaching, Candida loves Morell and tells him "put your trust in my love for you, James; for if that went, I should care very little for your sermons: mere phrases that you cheat yourself and others with everyday."[13] (Act II) For this vigorous criticism Candida has been criticized by many critics like A.M. Gibbs, who says, "Candida is indeed Morell's 'direst critic,' and she does much to upset his whole theory of himself."[14] In spite of all the comments of Candida directed upon Morell's life's work, he keeps on adoring her. Morell's persistent uxoriousness, despite assaulted comments of Candida, baffles critics.

Candida is pragmatic and practical, she knows the secret of Morell's success as a preacher. She knows the psychology of Proserpine and is competent enough to analyse the mental horizons of Eugene and her father Burgess as well. She tells Morell that all the women have "Prossy's complaint" (Act II) i.e. they are in love with Morell and are drawn towards him. Prossy can wash utensils because she is in love with her employer. Candida knows very well that Marchbanks has fallen in love with her and she wants to teach him the reality and truth of love. She knows how to control her father. Throughout the play she can be seen directing Morell, Marchbanks, Burgess, Prossy, Lexy and other characters of the play. It looks as if she were the axis and centre of energy and all are getting animated through her; she accomplishes what she wills. She makes Morell feel as the master of the house and never lets him feel inferior in front of others. She asks Marchbanks that James is master here. And after a few moments she says, "I make him master here, though he does not know it, and could not tell you a moment ago how it came to be so."[15] (Act III) Once again she calls Morell "master" but she holds the authoritative sway over him. If she can make him master she can make him aware of his weaknesses and shortcomings also. In the words of Barbara Bellow Watson:

> Candida thus does illustrate that kind of relationship in which a woman dedicates herself to the good of a man who needs her, and the man in turn does her the honor of supposing that the sacrifice is natural and joyful.... Having this easy management of the situation, she is able to do just as she pleases and yet remain, technically a woman of blameless conduct. Like Ann Whitefield, she can give a perfectly proper accounting for every improper thing she does.[16]

Candida knows Morell is completely under her control, and in the "Big Scene" she shows her sense of manipulation. When Morell asks her to choose anyone of them she gives a retort, "I suppose it is quite settled that I must belong to one or the other." (Act III) Her comment has a universal appeal as it alludes to the fate of helpless women who have no right to their own self. Marhbanks rightly recognises the underlying sense and says, "she means that she belongs to herself." (Act III) Candida emphatically announces, "I mean that and a good deal more.... My lords and masters, what have you to offer for my choice? I am up for auction..." (Act III) Candida justifiably selects Morell making him realise that he is the weaker of the two. She tells them that James Morell has been

> ...spoiled from his cradle.... Ask me what it costs to be James's mother and three sisters and wife and mother to his children all in one...when there is money to give, he gives it: when there is money to refuse, I refuse it. I build

> a castle of comfort and indulgence and love for him, and stand sentinel always to keep little vulgar cares out....[17] (Act III)

She substantiates that she is the focal point and James depends on her. Barbara Bellow Watson has written, "...Candida clearly feels that the character and accomplishments of her reverend husband have been plumped out by feeding on the energies of his mother, his sisters, and his wife."[18] Although she resents the spoon-feeding of her husband but not so much that can make her run out and slam the door of this ironical doll's house.

Candida's ambiguous treatment not only towards her husband but also towards Eugene Marchbanks raises some questions. What actually resides in her mind? If she is faithful to her husband, why a lover is permitted to build his little nest in the Morell's abode? But when it is the time of final decision she prefers Morell—why? Is she a flirt? Does she want to teach lessons of real love to both the male characters? Candida likes Marchbanks as she tells Morell, "Eugene's always right. He's a wonderful boy: I have grown fonder and fonder of him...he is ready to fall madly in love with me."[19] But she knows that the independent poetic, spirit of Marchbanks is "wild" which can prove pernicious to her future life. As Watson has observed, "Candida shows herself thoroughly practical. It does not matter that the poet is the strong one, for his independence of spirit is risky for a woman, as compared with the solid dependence of the Reverend Mr. Morell."[20]

As far as the relationship of Morell and Candida is concerned it is not love and hate relationship. The central point is not who loves whom but who loves whom and why? Candida loves Morell because he is strong in the society but weak before Candida. She loves Eugene because he is emotionally strong but weak before Candida. So both the men are weak before her; but Morell depends on her as she depends on him. It is not the case with Eugene, he does not depend on Candida and nor does she on him. He is, in the words of Morell, "one of the makers of the kingdom of heaven on earth...a master builder." (Act I) He knows "that it is in the poet that the holy spirit of man—the god within him—is more Godlike." (Act I) As Eric Bentley writes:

> The axis about which Candida revolves is that of strength and weakness, not love and hate...instead of the little woman reaching up towards the arms of the strong man, we have the strong woman reaching down to pick up her child.[21]

As Louis Crompton puts it:

> Candida, as a "Virgin Mother," is neither a conventional moralistic housewife nor a figure in the clouds. If the higher synthesis toward which Shaw sees Pre-Raphaelitism evolving includes both Morell's social concern and Eugene's libertarian views on love, Candida stands above both men by sharing something of the vision of each.[22]

And as Desmond MacCarthy puts it "Marchbanks has only been used to test the metal of others."[23] "A chance visitor" creates an upheaval in a happy marriage, shifting the universally lopsided scale and balancing it.

There are allegations against Candida that she is "immoral" and "prostitute." Shaw himself calls Candida, "immoral" and "as unscrupulous as Siegfried" in his letter to James Hunekar. This is a kind of appreciation of unconventionality and her freedom from false sentimentality. As Louis Crompton writes:

> Candida's unscrupulousness...comes in her willingness to exploit other people's sentimental feelings in order to further the practical management of the household...she regards the poet's love with maternal indulgence and regards heartbreak as one of the inevitable and healthy experiences of adolescence. Nor does her lack of scruples about her marriage vows matter. As Shaw puts it, Candida is 'straight for natural reasons, not for conventional ethical ones.'[24]

Whatever Candida does is quite "natural" and convincing.

Candida-Morell relationship has a bit of autobiographical touch like Shaw-Charlotte relationship. Just as Candida keeps all vulgar things out, in the same way Charlotte used to do for Shaw. Explaining the depth of their relation Michael Holroyd has observed:

> Charlotte treated her husband [Shaw] partly as an employer, partly as her child. It was the employer whose correspondence she dealt with, whose manuscripts she revised and took to the typist. She also arranged lunches with people he should meet and protected him from other people who would worry him needlessly.... But it was the child who exercised her talent for anxiety...[25]

Celestial bliss of Morell and Candida's married life gives a glimpse of Shaw and Charlotte's marital status. Beatrice Webb had said:

> Charlotte and Shaw have settled down into the most devoted married couple, she gentle and refined with happiness added thereto, and she showing no sign of breaking loose from her dominion. What the intellectual product of the marriage will be, I do not feel so sure.... It is interesting to watch his fitful struggles out of the social complacency natural to an environment of charm and plenty.[26]

The character of Candida has resemblances of Shaw's mother, Lucinda and Janet Achurah, a famous actress. "It [*Candida*] was to be their play, his and Janet's. It was to be their salvation together Candida derived from his mother and was to be replaced by Janet."[27] Shaw verbalises Janet's impression on him as Marchbanks utters Candida's influence upon him. Shaw has written, "Janet recreates me with an emotion which lifts me high out of that. I become a saint at once and write a drama in which I idealise Janet..."[28] Candida is modelled after Janet who "transport[s] them both to a plane of religious ecstasy."

Candida is one of the New Women created by Shaw. She does not have all the traits of a New Woman yet she has the biggest trait i.e. "self sufficiency." Like all the other New Women she is complacent; Shaw's women have a very ambivalent attitude and approach. Might be so because Shaw wants to amalgamate the tendencies of Victorian womanly woman with the susceptibilities of New Woman; in Candida we find this mixture. On the one hand she has affinities with Virgin Mother. Morell and Marchbaks idealize and desexualize her; on the other hand Candida is presented as a frankly sexual woman who "can manage people by engaging their affection, and who does so frankly and instinctively without the smallest scruple. So far, she is like any other pretty woman who is just clever enough to make the most of her sexual attractions for trivially selfish ends."[29] (Act I) To some extent Candida's character gives a peep into Shaw's psychology and his concept of women. Shaw's relationship with women was platonic without any direct involvement in any kind of physical pursuits yet he could never be fully free from the spell of their physical charm. All his women characters are charming and handsome irrespective of whether they are mothers or daughters.

When *Candida* was enacted on the stage it created a number of "Candidomaniacs" which really substantiates the phenomenal success of the play. It can be said in the words of Eric Bentley that the "charm of Candida" is more important than confusion and shortcoming.[30]

Another woman in this category is Barbara in the play *Major Barbara*. "Major," "A Romantic heroine," "Christ figure," "Instrument of Divine will" "Evangelist," Incarnation of "Apollonian will," "Ideal of sexual equality," "Salvationist and Reformer," "a Woman of Conscience," "Tempter and Cheapjack," all these are the descriptive epithets which describe the charismatic personality of one more Shavian woman.

Commenting on the universality of *Major Barbara* A.M. Gibbs in *The Art and Mind of Shaw* writes:

> Shaw achieves in *Major Barbara* a happy marriage of intellectually sophisticated and broadly popular ingredients. Like many of Shaw's characters, the romantic heroine cum Salvation Army Major, Barbara epitomizes a type, and has become part of the folk mythology of the twentieth century. Her successors in real life joined the Aldermaston rallies, or protested against the Vietnam war and apartheid in Africa, or left upper middle class homes to serve in organisations for the relief of suffering in the Third World.[31]

Such was the indelible impression of Shaw's Barbara.

The play *Major Barbara* inextricably revolves round a number of thematic concerns. Some critics visualize it as a perennial struggle between the individual and society. In the words of Purdom, the play is

> ...of conflict between the individual and society to which there is no resolution except by social redemption. The conflict arises over money, and Shaw puts members of the Salvation Army into the dilemma of accepting, for their work among the poor, money from a whisky distiller, and an armament manufacturer, or letting that work cease for want of funds. Major Barbara cannot reconcile herself to taking 'tainted money'; her colleague can. The dilemma makes a true dramatic theme, a theme of conscience, which becomes more than personal.[32]

Barbara is robuster, jollier, much more energetic in Salvation Army uniform. Introducing Barbara Lady Britomart remarks, "Ever since they made her a Major in the Salvation Army she has developed a propensity to have her own way and order people about which quite cows me sometimes. It's not lady like..."[33] (Act I) An initial introduction through these words installs Barbara as a lady of her own will and wish capable of exercising her authority and power. These words justify the title of the play *Major Barbara* showing the importance of woman. "It's not lady like" also testifies her willpower, single-mindedness, self-control and persistence. Commenting on this facet of her character, Margery M. Morgan in *The Shavian Playground* writes, "...the impression of the single figure in its stillness persists: there is strength of another kind in this maintained integrity and isolation. It is the apollonian will in Barbara that holds out now."[34] It is through the effect of this "apollonian will" that Barbara completes her "spiritual pilgrimage...through disillusion and despair to a rebirth of hope and a new vision."[35]

Barbara symbolizes eternal conscience of every human being. How this abstract, unobserved voice within is confronted with materialistic impressions, is the fundamental motive of the play and Shaw has been successful in his aim of establishing Barbara as a winner completely. The play deeply revolves round the problem of money and scarcity of it. The danger of poverty, of being poor is the most heinous crime and all other crimes are offshoots of this mother-of-all crime (The play opens with the discussion of money and ends with the discussion of money). G.K. Chesterton remarks:

> People say that poverty is no crime. Shaw says that poverty is a crime, that it is a crime to endure it, a crime to be content with it, that it is the mother of crimes of brutality, corruption and fear...that the crying need of the nation is not for better morals, cheaper bread, temperance, liberty, culture, redemption of fallen sisters and erring brothers, nor the grace, love and fellowship of the Trinity, but simply for enough money.[36]

As a Major of Salvation Army, Barbara has saved thousands of souls but only of the poor, scoundrels, criminals and infidels. Andrew Undershaft, her father, an arms-manufacturer and tycoon cut off from his children since their infancy is particularly attracted by his daughter, Barbara. Temperamentally and ideologically both are poles apart and challenge each other. Barbara invites Undershaft to the salvation shelter at the sign of the cross in Westham. Undershaft accepts her proposal for the visit provided that she will visit his works at the sign of the sword in Perivale St. Andres in Canning Town. Barbara challenges Undershaft that he would give up his business of cannons after having seen the work of Salvationists. Undershaft also forewarns her the same thing. At the salvation shelter, Undershaft maintains his composure. He believes that his arms-manufacturing trade is more effective in the task of soul-saving than the charitable activities of the Salvationists. When Barbara and her associates visit his works they internalise a cataclysmic change in their outlook. Barbara also feels an inner compulsion to judge her father's character. A critic's assessment is that, "Barbara the diehard is also forced to reassess her father's character when a financial crisis is reported in the Salvation Army."[37] There comes the climax of the conflict between mercenary Undershaft's principles and those of the soul saver Barbara's. Salvation Army is about to lose its existence as it has run out of money. Undershaft, ammunition-maker, and Lord Samundham, the manufacturer of Bodger's whisky, offer the required amount but the question is whether to take the tainted money for salvation or not! Barbara's faith gets a jolt and she tells her father:

> I stood on the rock I thought eternal; and without a word of warning it reeled and crumbled under me. I was safe with an infinite wisdom watching me, an army marching to salvation with me; and in a moment, at a stroke of your pen in a cheque book, I stood alone; and the heavens were empty.[38] (Act III)

Her pride is wounded to its core; she faces "the tragicomic irony of the conflict between real life and the romantic imagination."[39] Commenting on the individual soul's struggle with physical power Margery M. Morgan in *The Shavian Playground* writes:

> In this play Shaw grasped the basic nature of the threat offered to the intellect by the actual world; the challenge of undifferentiated force and mass in the physical universe to the essentially sole and individual; the ruthless and mindless violence that 'can destroy the higher power just as a tiger can destroy a man.'[40]

Disillusionment of Barbara gives her a higher pedestal than the earlier one:

> Barbara alone is the Christ figure of the play, its action represents her ministry, her betrayal and abandonment by her disciples, and her agony; leaving off the uniform of the Army is a kind of death; visiting the munitions factory of Undershaft and Lazarus, she harrows hell.[41]

Thus Barbara's personal emotional experience pressurizes her to recognise that the way of life lies through the factory of death and destruction has a proper place in the healthy scheme of things and religion and morality must change in order to survive. Her spirituality dies but her resurrection promises a new social order, a new brighter lease of life wherein she will be able to save everybody's soul without any class-difference. She realises the vicious circle of wealth in life.

Women in all the plays of Shaw come into a conflict with society and social norms directly and through their head-on collision; these women figures expose the follies and lacuna of social structure. They are not the prey of structural violence rather fight against it bravely. Writing about the inherent power in Shavian women Barbara Watson has observed:

> Shaw's women may collide disastrously with man-made institutions, as Major Barbara collides with the Salvation Army, Saint Joan with the Church, and Lysistrata in *The Apple Cart* with Breakages Ltd, but all these are right in their own terms. They are unworldly in respect of this man-made world of 'how it was done last time.' Therefore they are in trouble with the world, but not with the universe.[42]

In these plays *Major Barbara, Saint Joan, The Millionairess* Shaw has portrayed masterful women acting directly upon the world. Earlier he portrayed women who controlled a man's world by controlling men. Griffith considers them as "standard bearers of heroic unconventionality."[43]

Barbara is a medium to teach the gospel of socialism and Shaw's ethical approach to it. Gareth Griffith in *Socialism and Superior Brains* writes:

> Hatred of idleness and of poverty was the central motif of his socialism; their eradication, its denouement...socialism's first duty was to secure sufficiency of means for the masses. Financial security would be assured in the new economic order, an order when men would 'fight for ideas, not for bread and butter at one end and for corrupt domination and stolen luxury at the other.'[44]

Barbara is not a deserter, escaping the stark reality which shatters her divine mission. She admits before Cusins:

> I was happy in the Salvation Army for a moment. I escaped from the world into a paradise of enthusiasm and prayer and soul saving; but the moment our money ran short, it all came back to Bodger; it was he who saved our people: he, and the Prince of Darkness, my papa. Undershaft and Bodger: their hands stretch everywhere; when we feed a starving fellow creature, it is with their bread, because there is no other bread; when we tend the

> sick, it is in the hospitals they endow; if we turn from the churches they build, we must kneel on the stones of the streets they pave. As long as that last, there is no getting away from them. Turning our backs on Bodger and Undershaft is turning our backs on life.[45] (Act III)

Barbara accepts tainted money; nevertheless she maintains purity because she recognises that money is "only an environment for, not a creator of, spiritual values."[46] She does not surrender to Undershaft's values but identifies that the forces of evil and good cannot be separated but re-examined and remoulded. A.M. Gibbs writes:

> Barbara does not capitulate to Undershaft. Rather, she comes to a gradual recognition of the need to come to terms with the realities of his power. The moral imperatives on which the Army is based, and which Stephen in his different way espouses, are inadequate for dealing with the world as it is. Both Barbara and Cusins arrive at essentially the same recognition at the end of the play, that forces of evil must be not shunned but re-directed. Cusin's remark that 'you cannot have power for good without having power for evil too,' is in tune with the insights which Barbara is given a little further on in (Barbara's) final dialogue: There is no wicked side; life is all one.[47]

"Guardian Angel" Barbara knows and protects herself from being trapped by Undershaft's will. Her distancing of herself from her father Undershaft "a profiteer in mutilation and murder," (Act I) her independence and recovery of lost faith is indicated not in dialogue but in the action she takes.

> BARBARA. (hypnotised) Before I joined the Salvation Army. I was in my own power; and the consequence was that I never knew what to do with myself. When I joined it, I had not time enough for all the things I had to do.
>
> UNDERSHAFT. (approvingly) Just so, and why was that, do you suppose?

> BARBARA. Yesterday I should have said, because I was in the power of God. [She resumes her self-possession, withdrawing her hands from his with a power equal to his own].[48] (Act III)

Emphasising the effect of this gesture Gibbs writes:

> Undershaft's failure to hold Barbara in hypnotic sway shows that, unlike Dionysor in The Bacchae, he is not the wielder of ultimate power. By her withdrawal of her hands from him, Barbara shows that she is not the servant of Undershaft's will.[49]

Throughout the play there is continuous effort from Undershaft and Cusins to win Barbara which marks "sexual undercurrents" in Undershaft's relationship with Barbara.

> UNDERSHAFT. "Religion is our business at present, because it is through religion alone that we can win Barbara.
>
> CUSINS. Have you, too, fallen in love with Barbara.[50] (Act II)

Barbara's repossession of self and withdrawal of her hands from Undershaft's marks the beginning of the re-establishment of her adherence to Cusins, as well as an assertion of her independence.

Barbara's conversion to a new religion is the uppermost and superb part of her character. Desmond MacCarthy has analysed the difference between Barbara's old religion and her new:

> Barbara first lives in the religion of pity and humility, typified by the Salvation Army, which tries to save the world by spiritual methods alone. Then she finds that the influence of these methods depends ultimately upon the support of its enemies, of those whose fortunes are made out of the very miseries she tries to cure.... Then she begins to listen to the religion of her father. His is the religion of pride and self-reliance...to be strong...rich...and her last speech is the paean of her new religion 'I have got rid of the bribe of bread. I have got rid of the bribe of heaven. When I die let Him be in

> my debt, not I in His. Let God's will be done for its own sake. The work that he created us to do can only be done by living men and women.'[51]

Despite being the most prominent character in the play, Barbara has some serious flaws and analysing these Gibbs has said:

> Barbara's character in the play in fact shares some of the ambiguous qualities of Undershaft's. Overridingly, the impression she creates is radiant, vital and attractive. She is a woman of character and spirit who, in her active engagement with society's ills, contrasts in a favourable way with the utterly rigid Stephen and her female foil, the 'slender, bored and mundane' Sarah.... She is at times seen in a rather less favourable light. She is, for instance, presented in her treatment of Bill Walker as, like her father, a distinctly bossy and coercive person. There is a nagging quality about her attempts to convert Walker...diminish her stature.[52]

She definitely has a tendency to treat men like children. This matriarchal domineering nature she inherits from her mother Lady Britomart. At the end of the play Barbara turns out to be a baby figure:

> BARBARA. Yes: it is not easy work being in love with me, is it?...[she runs to the shed, and calls, childlike.] Mamma! Mamma! [Bilton comes out of the sheds followed by Undershaft] I want Mamma.
>
> ...
>
> LADY BRITOMART [coming from the shed...Barbara clutches like a baby at her mother's skirt]. Barbara: when will you learn to be independent and to act and think for yourself? I know as well as possible what that cry of "Mamma, Mamma," means. Always running to me![53] (Act III)

This episode minimises the grand impression of divine will epitomised by Barbara, the Salvation Army Major. Barbara—"the word means loveliness" (Act II) in the words of Cusins, ultimately returns to "loveliness." Her spiritual voyage completes with her turning back to life with a new religion of saving everybody's soul whether poor or rich, full-fed or ill-fed. This proves Shaw's faith in the ultimate goodness of women with which they can save the world. Barbara accepts the evils of society yet maintains her purity of conscience.

Lady Britomart, Mother of Major Barbara, is a woman of the world. A perfect example not only of a Shavian woman but of a Shavian Mother who upholds her own moral and ethical code of conduct yet rules and runs her family solely on her own terms. She mothers Barbara and her other children with a sense of difference between "right and wrong" (Act I) which helps them conquer the evil forces of the world. Emphasising this edifying aspect of a mother Margery M. Morgan in *The Shavian Playground* writes:

> It's [Lady Britomart's library] decorum, reflecting her own majestic rejection of all licence, is an essential adjunct to its perfect security; she herself prepared to recognise the dependence of the standards of a gentleman upon the tradition of classical education.[54]

Lady Britomart understands not only the value of moral and ethical rules but comprehends the reality of material need without which life is nothing but hell. She brings the matter of money in the minds of her children and makes them realise its need and requirement and the security it ensures to all the human beings. Margery M. Morgan writes:

> The whole play is flagrantly concerned with money...dominated by the opulent physical presence of Lady Britomart, laps us round in an atmosphere of womblike security. The unreality of material need and adversity...comes through all the more clearly for Lady Britomart's talk of economy...she is the abundant and never-failing earth-mother of the peak of the golden years. In explaining to Stephen their financial situation, she is merely eliciting the moral approval she thinks due to her; she knows the easy and comfortable, solution to her problems—such as they are!—and will apply it quite unscrupulously and without false pride; for she is free of the personal uncertainty that needs to worry about pride.[55]

A realistic and practical woman with farsightedness, Lady Britomart predominates in the beginning of the play. Her handling of her son Stephen and his subservient attitude to his mother exposes the maternal supremacy of the lady. Despite being a mother and a woman, she has a fatherly approach and control over her son and daughters. She gives them full freedom and independence to express their perceptions and plans yet there is an invisible rein which controls them throughout the play. Commenting on Lady Britomart's matriarchal domination Margery M. Morgan writes:

> She accuses him [Stephen—her son] of fiddling first with his 'tie,' then with his 'chain,' and the objects are certainly emblematic of his relations with her. The trick is later repeated in her scene alone with Undershaft:
>
> LADY BRITOMART. Andrew: You can talk my head off; but you can't change wrong into right. And your tie is all on one side. Put it straight.
>
> UNDERSHAFT (disconcerted). It won't stay unless it's pinned [he fumbles at it with childish grimaces].[56]

The power struggle between Undershaft and Lady Britomart to have control over the children comes to an end with the victory of Lady Britomart who feels dejected by the desertion of her children but ultimately gets her usual position by the return of Barbara to her. The victory of Lady Britomart is a reassertion of her authority and

> ...is a significant part of the emotional and thematic pattern of the play's close. Undershaft has had innumerable intellectual victories in the course of the play.... But Shaw's handling of the last scene of the play allows full weight to be given to Lady Britomart's strength of character, a strength which includes pragmatic and instinctive judgements about Undershaft to which it is impossible not to assent.[57]

Lady Britomart is also sometimes a comic figure. A.M. Gibbs analyses her comic spirit and says:

> Lady Britomart is a formidable figure in the play, and a vital component of its comic spirit and thematic structure. As a comic creation she is comparable in stature with Wilde's Lady Bracknell, and the comedy surrounding her, especially in the opening scene with Stephen, has a strongly Wildean flavour: 'Not break the law! He is always breaking the law. He broke the law when he was born: his parents were not married.' Shaw arms Lady Britomart with an unfailing rhetorical assurance, and great alacrity in seizing on the right moment for making discomforting remarks about personal mannerisms and disorderly dress. Her name recalls Spenser's female Knight of Chastity, and carries its later associations with militant, British female rectitude.[58]

Despite having an iron will Lady Britomart is susceptible and emotional. A.M. Gibbs thinks that she is presented as a domineering character, but also, at times, as emotionally vulnerable. Together with Stephen she expresses a view of morality which is quite different from Undershaft's—one in which the categories of right and wrong are indisputably clear and forever defined:

> STEPHEN. ...Right is right; and wrong is wrong; and if a man cannot distinguish them properly, he is either a fool or a rascal: that's all.
>
> LADY BRITOMART. [touched] That's my own boy [she pats his check]!...[59] (Act I)

It is also true that Lady Britomart plays no role in the Salvation Army or in Undershaft's empire and in the middle of the play she is reduced to a nonentity yet her efficiency in home management without her husband's presence and her sense of economy is worth appreciating. In the end her motives and plans of acquiring economic support for Barbara—Cusins, Stephen, Sara—Lomax work out. The main purpose with which the play opens is fulfilled at the end and in this way the play belongs to Lady. Emphasising the Britomart's presence Margery M. Morgan has written, "In retrospect, the action of the play, initiated by Lady Britomart, can be seen as the working-out of her purpose: to absorb and assimilate the potentially hostile forces, adding them to her own strength.[60]

Grace Tranfield is a widow, about thirty-two, slight of build, delicate of feature, and sensitive in expression and shows plenty of determination. Desmond MacCarthy calls Grace "a preliminary study for the superior women the dramatist afterwards drew."[61] Her sense of dressing is of superior level not of fashionable, trendy sort. She has no respect or concern for localism whether of dress or of language. Gareth Griffith in *Socialism and Superior Brains* says, "With respect to the issue of feminity, Shaw notes that Grace dresses without the slightest regard for fashion, 'though by no means with a careful concern for personal elegance'."[62] It insinuates that Shaw has never believed in dressing up a woman like a man to become a New Woman. There should be dignity and elegance in a woman by herself not as an imitator of man. Shaw here anticipates the modern feminists' notion of not mimicking male habits and dressing sense to get equality. A woman has her own distinct personal traits and she should exalt them and be proud to be a woman.

Grace calls herself a "New Woman" and to some extent this is true as she possesses some of the qualities which a New Woman is supposed to acquire. In her words, "No woman is the property of a man. A woman belongs to herself and to nobody else."[63] (Act I) She doesn't give way to emotions, does not get carried away by the susceptibilities and loving feeling of Charteris—her desired one. She asserts, "...I will never marry a man I love too much. It would give him a terrible advantage over me: I should be utterly in his power. That's what the New Woman is like."[64] (Act II) She exercises her wit and wisdom to retain not only her freedom and independence but also of every woman. During her conversation with Julia she scolds and rebukes her "when he [Charteris] is present to stand between us and play out the scene with you. I count for nothing. When we are alone, you fall back on your natural way of getting everything you want; crying for it like a baby until it is given to you."[65] (Act II) Grace rebukes Julia for degrading and deteriorating the position of women in the eye of man. "How I hate to be a woman when I see, by you, what wretched childish creatures we are!... Oh, if you had a scrap of self-respect...I understand now why Charteris has no respect for women."[66] (Act II) Grace's self-sufficiency and self-respect as a woman highlights the Ibsenite cult of independent unwomanly (not emotional) woman. She says, "...I will not give myself to any man who has learnt how to treat women from you and your like. I can do without his love, but not without his respect;..."[67] (Act II) A.M. Gibbs in *The Art and Mind of Shaw* is of the opinion that, "It is only in the persons of Grace Tranfield and the cheerful and independently minded younger sister of Julia Craven, Sylvia, that we see Ibsen discipleship in less adulterated form."[68]

The relationship between Grace and Charteris is that of rational comradeship and individual freedom. Both of them are fascinated and enthralled by each other yet they maintain their individuality. Charteris is in love with Grace because she is not a sentimental hog screaming, crying, and hankering after Charteris like Julia. Grace loves him and feels satisfied whenever Charteris shows that his exuberance and ultimate bliss depends on her. Grace, very well, knows how to impose her authority over Charteris without hunting or being hunted. She has a nonchalant approach towards Charteris in later part of the play. Charteris's non-committal approach to love sick woman makes her aware that he has no respect for women in love with him deeply. So she decides to remain friends with him ever after. Here she has similarities with Ibsen's Nora. "Grace's serious, level-headed and objective explanation to Charteris of her reasons for breaking off with him has easily recognisable affinities with Nora's dictation at the end of *A Doll's House*. Charteris had better keep on philandering."[69]

Grace resembles Prof. Higgins of *Pygmalion*. She needs a partner and believes in compatible co-existence, but not at the cost of servitude. For Grace there is something beyond the passion of love and that is personal freedom and the grace of being an independent woman, not in terms of economic condition but at physical as well as emotional level. She exposes the sentimental illusions of love to Julia and congratulates her at last "so you have shown him that you can do without him! Now I take back everything I said.... They think this a happy ending, Julia, our lords and masters!"[70] (Act III)

Grace, through her action of removing the blinkered altitude of Julia, has punished Charteris, and he gets nothing in hand neither Julia nor Grace. She makes him understand the value of a woman of substance and that women are not dolls to be played by him.

Grace has been criticised on many grounds and critics in their analysis, talk of her disparagingly. Sustaining her conviction of not marrying a person she loves too much, she evokes pity from audience and readers. She is a pitiable, wretched and an unfortunate character. Gareth Griffith indicates that "the new woman of the play and Julia's rival is a far more sympathetic character"[71] because she wins as a modern woman but loses as a woman.

Grace suppresses her emotion for the sake of her self-complacency, self-respect and a bit of self-protection. She brings in reason by suppressing her pent-up feelings. A.M. Gibbs sums up the strange predicament in which a New Woman may fall:

> ...Grace herself, in her rejection of Charteris seems to have arrived at a mainly negative solution to her predicament, in the suppression of passion: "I will never marry a man I love too much it would give him a terrible advantage over me: I should be utterly in his power. That's what the New Woman is like," the plays shows the New Woman as being trapped in a position of sterile neutrality, unwilling to accept both the attitudes of the philanderer and all the risks of entering into a fully committed, passionate relationship.[72]

Grace's decision anticipates Vivie Warren's decision to remain a spinster in *Mrs. Warren Profession*. Does Shaw mean a modern woman should extricate herself from the relationship of emotion? In fact by presenting a nonchalant attitude towards passionate, loving relationship Shaw wants to show that women are not emotional fools. They should have reason behind everything whether love or marriage. There should be compatibility, equality of everything. Relationship should not be lopsided where woman is disparaged.

Strong-minded women in this chapter have got the "unbending quality of saints and martyrs—a quality based on their immoderate assurance of being right against all opposition and all evidence."[73] These saving women are invincible and protected by a kinder providence. They have not only the power to save, and thus be saviours but are courageous and capable to loving.

REFERENCES

1. Barbara Bellow Watson, *A Shavian Guide to the Intelligent Woman*, (London: Chatto and Windus, 1964), p. 165.
2. *Ibid*, p. 164.
3. *Ibid*, p. 167.
4. Margery M. Morgan, *The Shavian Playground: An Exploration of the Art of George Bernard Shaw*, (London: Methuen and Co. Ltd., 1974), pp. 65-66.
5. Gail Finney, *Women in Modern Drama: Freud, Feminism and European Theatre at the Turn of the Century*, (London: Cornell University Press, 1989), p. 187.
6. *Ibid*.
7. Sigmund Freud, "Femininity" ("Die Weiblichheit"), Se, XXII, pp. 133-134 as quoted in Gail Finney, *Women in Modern Drama. Freud, Feminism and European Theatre at the Turn of the Century*, p. 187.
8. Gail Finney, *Women in Modern Drama: Freud, Feminism and European Theatre at the Turn of the Century*, p. 189.
9. George Bernard Shaw, *Candida*, ed. S. Sengupta, (New Delhi: Subject Publications, 1980), p. 20.
10. *Ibid*, p. 46.
11. Margery M. Morgan, *The Shavian Playground: An Exploration of the Art of George Bernard Shaw*, p. 74.
12. *Candida*, p. 53.
13. *Ibid*.
14. A.M. Gibbs, *The Art and Mind of Shaw: Essays in Criticism*, (London: The Macmillan Press Ltd, 1983), p. 81.
15. *Candida*, p. 79.
16. Barbara Bellow Watson, *A Shavian Guide to the Intelligent Woman*, p. 67.
17. *Candida*, pp. 78-79.
18. Barbara Bellow Watson, *A Shavian Guide to the Intelligent Woman*, p. 66.
19. *Candida*, p. 51.
20. Barbara Bellow Watson, *A Shavian Guide to the Intelligent Woman*, p. 67.
21. Eric Bentley, "The Making of a Dramatist (1892-1903)," R.J. Kaufmann, ed., *G.B. Shaw: A Collection of Critical Essays*, (New Jersey: Prentice-Hall, 1965), p. 71.
22. Louis Crompton, *Shaw the Dramatist: A Study of the Intellectual Background of the Major Plays*, (London: George Allen and Unwin Ltd., 1971), p. 42.

23 Desmond MacCarthy, *SHAW*, (London: Macgibbon and Kee, 1995), p. 24

24. Louis Crompton, *Shaw the Dramatist: A Study of the Intellectual Background of the Major Plays*, p. 42.

25. Michael Holroyd, *Bernard Shaw: The Pursuit of Power*, Vol. II, 1898-1918, (London: Chatto and Windus, 1989), p. 58.

26. *Ibid*, p. 10.

27. Michael Holroyd, *Bernard Shaw: The Search for Love*, Vol. I, 1866-1998, (London: Chatto and Windus, 1988), p. 315.

28. *Ibid*.

29. *Candida*, pp. 19-20.

30. Eric Bentley, "The Making of a Dramatist (1892-1903)," R.J. Kaufmann, ed., *G.B. Shaw: A Collection of Critical Essays*, (New Jersey: Prentice-Hall, 1965), pp. 69-70.

31. A.M. Gibbs, *The Art and Mind of Shaw: Essays in Criticism*, p. 153.

32. C.B. Purdom, *A Guide to the Plays of Bernard Shaw*, (London: Methuen, 1963), p. 208.

33. George Bernard Shaw, *Major Barbara*, ed. S. Sengupta, (New Delhi: Surjeet Publications, 1979), p. 57.

34. Margery M. Morgan, *The Shavian Playground: An Exploration of the Art of George Bernard Shaw*, pp. 143-144.

35. *Ibid*.

36. *Major Barbara*, pp. 176-177.

37. *Ibid*, p. 172.

38. *Ibid*, p. 145.

39. C.B. Purdom, *A Guide to the Plays of Bernard Shaw*, p. 209.

40. Margery M. Morgan, *The Shavian Playground: An Exploration of the Art of George Bernard Shaw*, p. 136.

41. *Ibid*, p. 144.

42. Barbára Bellow Watson, *A Shavian Guide to the Intelligent Woman*, p. 68.

43. Gareth Griffith, *Socialism and Superior Brains: The Political Thought of Bernard Shaw*, (London: Routledge, 1993), p. 176.

44. *Ibid*, pp. 28-29.

45. *Major Barbara*, p. 157.

46. A.M. Gibbs, *The Art and Mind of Shaw: Essays in Criticism*, p. 159.

47. *Ibid*, pp. 161-162.

48. *Major Barbara*, pp. 144-145.
49. A.M. Gibbs, *The Art and Mind of Shaw: Essays in Criticism*, p. 164.
50. *Major Barbara*, p. 96.
51. *Ibid*, p. 56.
52. A.M. Gibbs, *The Art and Mind of Shaw: Essays in Criticism*, pp. 160-161.
53. *Major Barbara*, p. 159.
54. Margery M. Morgan, *The Shavian Playground: An Exploration of the Art of George Bernard Shaw*, p. 140.
55. *Ibid*, p. 148.
56. *Ibid*, p. 153.
57. A.M. Gibbs, *The Art and Mind of Shaw: Essays in Criticism*, pp. 164-165.
58. *Ibid*, p. 165.
59. *Major Barbara*, p. 55.
60. Margery M. Morgan, *The Shavian Playground: An Exploration of the Art of George Bernard Shaw*, p. 153.
61. Desmond MacCarthy, *SHAW*, p. 82.
62. *The Philanderer*, p. 168.
63. George Bernard Shaw, *"The Philanderer", in Bernard Shaw: Complete Plays with Prefaces*, vols. I-VI, (New York: Dodd Mead & Co., 1962), p. 729.
64. *Ibid*, p. 767.
65. *Ibid*, p. 781.
66. *Ibid*.
67. *Ibid*.
68. A.M. Gibbs, *The Art and Mind of Shaw: Essays in Criticism*, p. 66.
69. *Ibid*.
70. *The Philanderer*, p. 800.
71. Gareth Griffith, *Socialism and Superior Brains: The Political Thought of Bernard Shaw*, p. 167.
72. A.M. Gibbs, *The Art and Mind of Shaw: Essays in Criticism*, p. 67.
73. Barbara Bellow Watson, *A Shavian Guide to the Intelligent Woman*, p. 169.

5

Heroic Woman

Joan is a country girl of seventeen, unladylike and uncommon, "enlightened by her visions and transformed by faith," with an inborn courageous conscience to convince all men. Shaw's main purpose in the creation of Joan's character is to represent a heavenly spirit conflicting and struggling with the ephemeral and worldly powers constituting religion and state. In other words, as A.C. Ward has written:

> The conflict between Joan of Arc and the Christian church was a conflict between Private Judgement and Constituted Authority; and, this being so, the political leaders also became alarmed, for they saw that their authority, too, would be in danger.[1]

The essence of the theme is projected in the controversial epilogue in which Joan's victory shows the perennial and ongoing struggle of independent religious inspiration against established religions, against the patriot, the statesman and the most powerful and strongest of them—the Catholic Church. Although Joan as a girl is not like other women characters who remain victorious in the end yet she should not be considered a wretched, pathetic, defeated woman. She should be taken as a valiant, courageous woman who sacrificed her life for the great cause of religion. As Purdom has written, "The maid should be treated not as a sentimental heroine, but as a heroic character martyred for her faith...[2]

In 1920 Joan of Arc was at last canonized by Pope Benedict XV. This decision of the church, as Valency has written, "reflected church policy with respect to the post-war resurgence of faith in Catholic countries."[3] In France, Joan had played a significant part in the war effort. Just before her canonization in 1920, France was gradually recovering from the burden of the German invasion during the 1914-1918 war. During that period of crisis the French recollected the deeds of Saint Joan and her memory strengthened and uplifted their morale. Her story revitalized their courage. She was seen on posters fighting magnificently in the trenches alongside her poilus. She was an invaluable symbol of French military prowess. Her belated canonization gave Shaw the golden moment to write on a subject which had captured his imagination long ago; he mentioned it in a letter (written from Orleans in 1913) to Stella Campbell that the story of Joan of Arc had created a warm interest in him. He informed her that he would write a Joan play some day, "beginning with the sweeping up of the cinders and orange peel after her martyrdom, and going on with Joan's arrival in heaven."[4]

Exactly ten years later, in 1923, Shaw was writing about Saint Joan with the same motivation of taking her to heaven. Sydney Cockerell, curator of the Fitzwilliam Museum at Cambridge, suggested to him that there might be a play on it. Mrs. Shaw was also deeply interested and she contrived to keep the subject warm until Shaw started writing on it.

Shaw recaptured the historical figure of St. Joan and recast her emphasizing certain writers who portrayed her in various manners. Joan's character had undergone several changes since making her appearance in Shakespeare's Henry VI as a "trull," "witch," "strumpet," "foul fiend of France."[5] In the eighteenth century she was transformed by Schiller and Southey (as well as by Verdi and Tchaikovsky) from being "an agent of foreign devils" into a popular liberator and nationalist heroine; yet her character was made to appear as a creature of romance and melodrama. Shaw viewed Tom Taylor's heroic historical pageant play *Jeanne d'Arc* but was remorseless for the impossibility of serious character study. He felt that she had been exploited by Voltaire also. Voltaire used her in his mock Homeric epic *La Pucelle* to comment ridiculously on everything that he justifiably hated in the institutions and fashions of his own day. Antole France also misused her in his *Vie*. Mark Twain exploited her romantically who converted her into an unblemished American school teacher in armor. Andrew Lang presented her sentimentally as a beautiful and most lady-like Victorian. Shaw wrote, "I love the real Joan...but the conventional Joan of the stage makes me sick."[6]

In this "medieval visionary" Shaw recognised, says Michael Holroyd:

> The simplicity of spirit needed for the regeneration of society in the modern world...[she] possesses a superior power—what he called in *Peace Conference Hints* 'the entirely mystic force of evolution applied through the sort of living engine' we call the man of principle.[7]

In this way Shaw attempted to mould her as "the vehicle for a living dialogue between ancient and modern worlds."[8] Shaw, in fact, utilized the ancient figures to represent modern ideas and perceptions in vogue. On this creative ability of Shaw, Desmond MacCarthy has written that the first and foremost act Shaw undertakes, when his setting is in the past, is to:

> ...rub off his period the patina of time...; he will scrub and scrub till contemporary life begins to gleam through surface strangeness and oddities. He is confident that he has reached historic truth when he has succeeded in scratching historic characters till he finds beneath a modern man in fancy dress.[9]

In the preface to *Saint Joan Shaw* introduces the original and audacious Joan:

> Joan of Arc, a village girl of the Vosges, was born about 1412; burnt for heresy, witchcraft, and sorcery in 1431; rehabilitated after a fashion in 1456; designated venerable in 1904; declared Blessed in 1908; and finally canonized in 1920. She is the most notable Warrior Saint in the Christian calendar, and the queerest fish among the eccentric worthies of the Middle Ages. Though a professed and most pious Catholic, and the projector of a Crusade against the Husites, she was in fact one of the

> first apostles of Nationalism...she was the pioneer of rational dressing for women...she refused to accept the specific woman's lot, and dressed and fought and lived as men did.[10]

Shaw has built his Joan after this presumption as the first Protestant martyr, apostle of Nationalism and the pioneer of manly woman who lived like man. These are the three main aspects to the character of Saint Joan, which Shaw has highlighted. We shall be discussing these three characteristics along with some others in detail.

Joan's innocence, youthfulness, confidence are discernible in the midst of the play's various experienced, grown-up, well-thought-out personalities. She is the most superlatively imagined figure with multifaceted facets. She has the amalgamation of ingenuousness and occasional naivete with quick-wittedness and great common sense. On observing closely one gets the idea that her innocence works as sixth sense which even the most sane people cannot boast to have. She is described as:

> An able bodied country girl of 17 or 18, ...with an uncommon face: eyes very wide apart and bulging as they often do in very imaginative people, a long well-shaped nose with wide nostrils, a short upper lip, resolute...mouth, and handsome fighting chin.[11] (Scene I)

Her voice is a hearty coaxing voice, very confident, very appealing, irresistible. Her countenance and sturdy physic emphasises her earthiness. "The outrageousness of Joan's claims and intentions," in the words of Arnold Silver, "would be intolerable were it not for the force of her personality, 'her magnetic field' as Shaw termed it in a stage direction."[12] She is dauntless, bold and confident about everything and this confidence she derives from her sense of servitude to God. Her first few words give a clear picture of this aspect:

> JOAN [bobbing a curtsey]. Good morning, captain squire. Captain you are to give me a horse and armor and some soldiers, and send me to the Dauphin. Those are your orders from my Lord.[13] (Scene I)

She thinks that she is the messenger of God on the earth and this divine power gives her immense assurance, boldness and courage. She claims that God has sent her to raise the siege of Orleans.

> ROBERT (flabbergasted). To raise the siege of Orleans!
>
> JOAN (simply). Yes, squire: that is what God is sending me to do. Three men will be enough for you to send with me...they have promised to come with me. Polly and Jack and-[14] (Scene I)

Joan calls the bigwigs by nicknames and the unintentional brazen attitude certainly arouses a fascination towards her. This blend of innocence and confidence to fulfil the heaven-sent mission is really enthralling. In fact she could be dismissed as an ignorant, strolling village idiot, but two aspects of her personality help to establish the truthfulness of her motive. First one is her "knack of restoring men's faith in themselves and the odd way nature behaves when she passes by..."[15] Hens start laying eggs and the west wind starts blowing after a long absence. All these factors remove the scepticism not only of Robert and other dramatis personae but of spectators and readers as well as those who start reposing their faith in Joan.

Joan has visions and voices to direct her. These visions and voices lead her towards heavenly goal. She tells Dunois:

> It is in the bells I hear my voices... Do you hear? "Dear-child-of-God"; just what you said. At the half-hour they will say "Be-brave-go on." ... But it is at the hour, when the great bell goes after "God-will-save-France": It is then that St. Margaret and St. Catherine and sometimes even the blessed Michael will say things that I cannot tell beforehand.[16] (Scene V)

Shaw rationalises Joan's voices in the preface to the play. Due to them she is held first to be a liar, an impostor, a sorceress and the instrument of Prince of Darkness and after centuries as a "Saint." Shaw comments on the matter-of-fact historians and their circumscribed discerning sense of reading people's minds. There are a few people whose power of imagination is so vivid that ideas come to them in the form of an audible voice and sometimes spoken by a visible figure. Socrates, Luther, Swedenborg, Blake had visions and heard voices just as Saint Francis and Saint Joan did. Thus Joan is not insane but a sane woman in spite of her voices.[17] Michael Holroyd writes that Shaw has "Shavianized" Joan's voices by interpreting them as "evidence of living imagination—'the inspirations and institutions and unconsciously reasoned conclusions of genius' which are miraculous...because of exceptional consequences."[18] In fact the instinct which manifests itself as voices and visions in the case of Joan, driving her to take actions impulsively, works with Shaw also inspiring him to write. Ten years earlier, before writing the play, he had explained "I am pushed by a natural need to set to work to write down the conversations that come into my head unaccountably.... At first I hardly know the speakers.... Finally I...discover...." By this "telepathic process of 'sane hallucination' " Shaw expected to acclimatize himself with Joan.[19] Shaw explained to his American Manager Lawrence Langner that the play was written under the direct inspiration of Joan of Arc. He said, "As I wrote, she guided my hand, and the words came tumbling out at such speed that my pen rushed across the paper and I could barely write fast enough to put them down."[20] Valency has written that if this is the truth one can only "marvel at the literary aptitude of his saintly muse."[21]

The tragedy of Joan centres around only three things and at last these things pave the way for her sainthood. Being a Catholic, she is the first Protestant martyr. Desmond MacCarthy has written that the play is an "exceedingly powerful protestant pamphlet [and], the essence of Protestantism being reliance upon internal authority...as against the authority of tradition and a corporate religion which also claim inspiration."[22] Joan's indomitable faith in her voices directing her to accomplish the work assigned by God symbolizes one's own conscience guiding her towards a better religion than the prevalent religion with flaws. During the course of the play she follows her voices without being impertinent to the Churchmen consciously. She believes innocently that Church officials would help her in her mission because she is the "servant of God" and the Church is the symbol of God on earth. So if the Church helps her, it will support God's will. Shaw has written in the preface that "it is always hard for superior wits to understand the fury roused by their exposures of the stupidities of comparative dullards."[23] Joan innocently thinks that she is serving God in the same way as the Church is serving God, but in reality she prepares her rivals and enemies. She asks Dunois:

> JOAN. Why do these countries and knights and churchmen hate me?... I have asked nothing for myself...I have crowned Charles and made him a real king;....
>
> DUNOIS. [rallying her] Sim-ple-ton! Do you expect stupid people to love you for showing them up?... Do ambitious politicians love the climbers who take the front seats from them? Do archbishops enjoy being played off their own altars, even by saints?....[24] (Scene V)

Joan thinks that "minding your own business is like minding your own body:...it is God's business we are here to do: not our own..."[25] (Scene II) and she proclaims bravely before everyone that, " I am sent to you to drive the English away from Orleans and from France, and to crown you [Dauphin] king in the Cathedral of Rheims."[26] (Scene II) It is her strong faith in God and her strong conviction to follow the orders of God that she falls from the grace of high and mighty people. She thinks that she is "a faithful child of the Church" (Scene VI) and will obey the church provided it does not order for impossible things. She never conforms to the command that says her visions and revelations are not from God. Whatever God makes her do she will never go back on it. Hence she impudently declares in the public:

> JOAN. I believe that God is wiser than I; and it is His commands that I will do. All the things that you call my crimes have come to me by the order of God: it is impossible for me to say anything else. If any churchman says the contrary I shall not mind him; I shall mind God alone, whose command I always follow.[27] (Scene VI)

It is her impetuous and pert answer that "God must be served first" which defames her as "heretic" i.e. not serving the church. She upholds that her voices do not tell her to "disobey the church but God must be served first." (Scene VI) Here begins the difference between Catholic faith and Protestant faith. In the middle ages who ever went against church was considered to be evil-spirited. There was no other religion than following the Catholic Church. They believed the voices and visions to be diabolic in their attempt to demolish the supremacy of the Catholic Church. Shaw has written in the preface that Joan was in a state of invincible ignorance as to the Church's view; and the Church could not tolerate her pretensions without either waiving its authority or giving her a place beside the Trinity during her life-time and in her teens, which was unthinkable. Thus an "irresistible force met an immovable obstacle, and developed the heat that consumed poor Joan."[28] In the play Joan's following her instincts ardently is interpreted as "heresy." D'estivet says "assuredly, if you are in the hands of the Church, and you wilfully take yourself out of its hands, you are deserting the Church; and that is heresy."[29] (Scene VI) What was "heresy" at that time came to be known as "Protestant belief" in later period and on account of this Joan was canonized as Saint and entitled as "the first Protestant" by the literary men and historians. Joan's own religion is an allusion to Shaw's interpretation of religion. The essay "Bernard Shaw and London Heretics" highlights his religious sentiment:

> Since there was no affirmative religion in the western world in which a reasonably intelligent man could believe, Shaw proceeded to devise one for himself. He enjoyed using old words in fresh ways and one can find him calling himself a Catholic at one point and a Protestant at another. He used the word Catholic to mean universal (it meant the same as communist, he said). When he called himself protestant, he thought of himself as separatist from the Establishment.... His aim, therefore, was a belief that could be at the same time individual and universal.... Shaw preferred a mystical revelation to a rationalist one.[30]

Shaw always appreciated the people who assessed the values independently without following them blindfold. He admired people who were "Catholics as members of a community in economic and social matters but Protestant in matters of relationship with God,"[31] a highly personal relationship based on one's intuitive powers. Joan is an extension of this amalgamation of Catholic and Protestant viewpoints.

Joan is regarded as a nationalist because she persistently holds the view that God has given France to the French and England to the English. She continuously asks the questions like who has given the English rights to siege the land of the French:

> JOAN. They [the English] are only men. God made them just like us; but He gave them their own country and their own language; and it is not His will that they should come into our country and try to speak our language.[32] (Scene I)

Joan inspires the French army to be courageous to fight against the English. She instils the sense of being French into their minds. Her nationalistic spirit reawakens the spirit of French army. This proves dangerous to the devious English rulers, feudal lords and the authority of the Church. The following dialogue between the Nobleman and the Chaplain gives an idea of the hazardous results of sprouting nationalism:

> THE NOBLEMAN. A Frenchman! Where did you pick up that expression? Are these Burgundians and Bretons...beginning to call themselves Englishmen? They actually talk of France and England as their countries. Theirs, if you please! What is to become of me and you if that way of thinking comes into fashion?
>
> THE CHAPLAIN. Why my lord? Can it hurt us?
>
> THE NOBLEMAN. Men cannot serve two masters. If this cant of serving their country once takes hold of them, goodbye to the authority of their feudal lords, and goodbye to the authority of the church. That is, goodbye to you and me.[33] (Scene IV)

In the words of Cauchon, it can be assumed that "...to her the French speaking people are what the Holy Scriptures describe as a nation. Call this side of her heresy Nationalism..."[34] (Scene IV) Thus Joan's "secular heresy" has two facets—Protestantism and Nationalism. This is the reason that, in the words of Warwick, "her death [becomes] a political [and religious] necessity."[35] (Scene VI)

Joan undoubtedly pressurises and persuades French soldiers lifting them out of their ignorance of war strategies. The real miracle, as Michael Holroyd has observed, happens off-stage and this is Joan's rectification of the French army. A new spirit rises in men when Joan inspires them. They find themselves at the onset of a new era and "Joan represents the dawning of this new spirit of nationalism."[36] The miracle is in the belief which Joan creates and which makes the soldiers follow Joan and her doctrine of France for the French with fatalistic confidence.

The reformation, in the words of Valency, definitely waited for the arrival of Luther but from Shaw's standpoint, Joan was the precursor of both Protestantism and Nationalism. It is chiefly because of their "premonition of the coming danger that the nobility, in the person of Warwick, and the prelacy, in the person of Cauchon, reluctantly resolve that the maid must be discredited and destroyed."[37] But the burning of Joan did not check the progress of history and within a quarter-century of her death, both the church and the state discovered her righteousness and her orthodoxy. In this way she became a symbol of progress and Warwick, Cauchon became the symbol of the reactionary forces of their time. Thus the play in these terms fitted admirably into Shaw's philosophic scheme.[38]

Shaw goes one step ahead of all these notions against Joan. He, in the preface, clarifies that Joan was not tried as a political offender. "Ecclesiastical courts and the courts of the inquisition...were courts Christian: that is international courts; and she was tried, not as traitress, but as a heretic, blasphemer, sorceress and idolater."[39] Charges levelled against her were not political offences against England, nor against France but against God and against the common morality of Christendom. The idea of nationalism was so exotic and alien to the medieval conception of Christian society that it might almost have been directly charged against Joan as an additional heresy.[40] This is the thing which Shaw has tried to project in the play and she is burnt on this basis. She actually does not have the least idea of the charges she is accused of. Her piety seems superhuman to the formally dutiful people who follow religion as their duty.

Joan is the precursor not only of nationalism and Protestantism, but she is also the first woman warrior. Shaw has written in the preface that:

> Joan's campaigning could not have been carried on in petticoats. This was not only because she did a man's work, but because it was morally necessary that sex should be left out of the question as between her and her comrades-in-arms.[41]

Joan has been portrayed as a woman of action unlike other homely women. She is addressed by La Hire "a girl in armor, like a soldier." (Scene II) This was something incredible in medieval ages. The Archbishop condemns her:

> ARCHBISHOP. This creature is not a saint. She is not even a respectable woman. She does not wear women's clothes. She is dressed like a soldier, and rides round the country with soldiers....[42] (Scene II)

Joan is a born warrior, inclined to soldiering since her childhood, likes riding a horse, wearing soldier's outfits and dress and loves fighting. She has, as Dunois foresees it, "the makings of a soldier...[and she is] in love with war." (Scene III) She is born to set her country free of invaders. She ventures to achieve what seems to be an uphill task to the veteran warriors of army. She does not care for people even when they call her a sorceress, a witch. She is very rash, hasty and impetuous. Immediately after meeting Dunois, in the third scene, she plans to attack English soldiers. She does not care whether her soldiers follow her or not. She knows the weakness of French soldiers who fight to take ransoms and are chicken-hearted; they do not face the enemy courageously. She delivers many French soldiers from fear and they fight valiantly for the freedom of their nation, to free it from English bondage.

In the preface to the play "Shaw likens Joan to the type of Militant female. At the court as well as in the camp, she is a gadfly, an earnest, urgent woman of mannish cut, logical, businesslike, and efficient in the pursuit of her goals."[43] Joan is actually an advanced version of Vivie Warren, "ritually pure," fully dedicated to her mission with no nonsense about her. Michael Holroyd writes that Shaw has made her "the heroic example of an undiscovered modern leader, the warrior-saint he had sometimes thought of dramatizing as Cromwell and Mahomet, and had looked for in a play about the unknown soldier."[44]

Joan is a born boss—a purposeful young woman who enjoys taking change and ruling over men instead of being ruled over. In the words of Arnold Silver "she is the latest and the youngest, in a long line of Shavian managerial women, going back to Blanche Sartorius of his first play, *Widowers' Houses*."[45] She cuts her hair short and wears soldier's outfits to lessen the awareness of her feminity. Although the Chaplain insists on emphasising her womanly attributes, like shedding tears when in pain, Joan declares, "...I am a soldier: I do not want to be thought of as a woman. I will not dress as a woman.... They dream of lovers, and of money. I dream of leading a charge, and of placing the big guns...."[46] (Scene III) She dislikes a woman's garb. This is again an androgynous approach representing Shaw's philosophy of sexual equality.

Joan is representative of young generation wherein boyish females, now, are not exceptions. She possesses the typical qualities of youth struggling against the world of adults. She has wilfulness, brashness, impatience with customary procedures and rebelliousness revolting for experimental and innovative ideas which the modern youth have to form their personal life in accordance with their intuitive conscience. Emphasising this aspect of her character Arnold Silver has written:

> The younger spectators in the audience can feel her to be a surrogate in their current conflict with their elders, and the older spectators can feel stirrings of their own buried rebellions against authority figures: in the darkened theatre, with the make-believe enacted before us, we all become adolescents identifying with this fearless teenager.[47]

Joan, like all the other women characters in the Shavian canon, matures in terms of worldly cognizance. At the very outset she is inexperienced but as she goes through the roller-coaster ride of life replete with political and religious restraints, she understands the real and practical world. Once President Woodrow Wilson said that when men attain power they either "swell" or "grow." Joan, having acquired success and power, she certainly grew. This growth is visible by the fifth scene, when she does not remain the same innocent, and submissive girl as she is shown in the beginning. She is aware of the devious nature of the world and realizes that courtly people will be happy seeing her burn. "The innocent girl is turning into a disillusioned woman"[48] and Shaw has given fine touches in the coexistence of both the phases in her. Joan's developing maturity gives her more confidence and this 'swelling of the ego,' engendered by her success in fighting, makes her feel free to give advice to kings and generals, and she declares to Dunois: "you don't know how to begin a battle; and you don't know how to use your cannons. And I do."[49] (Scene V) She now speaks disparagingly and downplays everyone. She speaks to the Archbishop of Rheims insultingly before whom she had humbly knelt on her first visit to the court. She declares that, "you are not fit that I should live among you." (Scene VI) Dunois accuses Joan of thinking that she has "God in her Pocket." (Scene V) The Archbishop rebukes her and specifies her flaw that "you came clothed with the virtue of humility; [and now]...you have stained yourself with the sin of pride. The old Greek tragedy is rising among us. It is the chastisement of hubris."[50] (Scene V) Yet her pride is not hubris. Shaw wants to inject some human imperfections into Joan, in order to provide a full balance, to show that in the charge of presumptuousness that is levied against, there is some justice. She has some vanity and is little bit puffed up with her success: she could be more faithful and mannerly. She feels proud in serving God truthfully and accumulating honours He has brought her. Here *Saint Joan* resembles the Greek play *Antigone*, for the heroine of that literary piece also defies earthly powers to obey religious obligations and she shows firmness rather than excessive pride. Thus we can say that Joan's "fundamental sin," according to the Churchmen of the trial, is not hubris but heresy. They see her as "doctrinally defying the Church—its authority and instructions. She sees herself as obeying supreme religious imperatives."[51] Her death results from virtues, excesses of piety. In this way she represents for Shaw the principle of Christianity without a church, or of a church reserved for only secondary, social purposes. In the epilogue it is said of her: "The girls in the field praise thee; for thou hast raised their eyes; and they see that there is nothing between them and heaven."[52]

Shaw felt that Joan's story was ideally suited to his realist purpose and thus *Saint Joan* became his passion play. There are some affinities between Jesus Christ and Saint Joan; the latter represents another coming of Christ to the world. Both of them are heroes as victims transformed into saviours. Like Jesus, Joan is also "an agent for change religiously inspired against the idealist status quo of established Church."[53] Chauchon cries out—"Must then a Christ perish in torment in every age to save those that have no imagination?"[54] His sympathetic words make the connection between Jesus and Joan clear. She herself says, "...I am His child, and you are not fit that I should live among you...."[55] (Scene VI) Joan is far more real than Jesus because she defends herself splendidly, wiping the floor with her accusers every time. Jesus was never a struggler and he bore all the pain afflicted on him silently.[56]

Saint Joan transformed Bernard Shaw also as Bernard Levin commented that "she was the only woman who ever managed to wipe the smirk from Shaw's face,"[57] and this was her "final miracle." Johan Huizinga claimed that Joan brought Shaw "to his knees" with such reverence which is certainly a kind of conversion. The conversion of meek mild Dauphin from being a chicken hearted prince to Charles the Victorious is a distinct parallel of Sony's (Shaw's childhood name) conversion into G.B.S., from a "sickly coward to potential leader."[58] Shaw used middle-aged Fabian Mary Hankinson as a model for Saint Joan although critics such as Maurice Valency and others find no resemblance between them.[59] Through Joan, Shaw has given a vivid picture of the evolution of human being from immaturity to maturity; how Life Force keeps on fulfilling its desire of designing better human beings. Valency has written that Shaw wished to write a

> ...tragedy with universal connotations. Joan, in her sacred aspect is, accordingly, a spectacular realization of the Life Force, a genius precariously balanced on the threshold of the future, and therefore especially vulnerable to the forces of reaction.[60]

The story of Saint Joan is not simply a tragedy of a girl—but "the eternal agony of a race that burns its saints."[61] We have seen that Shaw's women characters are rebels who fight against the established order and are therefore particularly vulnerable in the hands of its defenders.

Shaw's world is full of women: some are to be loved, some to be respected and others to be feared. He could never get tired of discussing them and he always liked to have a woman as his central character. It was a subject dear to his heart and as vast as religion in its scope of discussion. Thus *Saint Joan* gave him an opportunity to combine woman with religion for the expression of his progressive ideas at the highest level.

REFERENCES

1. George Bernard Shaw, *Saint Joan*, ed., A.C. Ward, (Hyderabad: Orient Longman Ltd., 1995), p. 199.
2. C.B. Purdom, *A Guide to the Plays of Bernard Shaw*, (London: University Paperbacks, Methuen, 1963), p. 284.
3. Maurice Valency, *The Cart and the Trumpet: The Plays of George Bernard Shaw*, (New York: Oxford University Press, 1973), p. 369.
4. Michael Holroyd, *Bernard Shaw: The Lure of Fantasy*, Vol-III, 1918-1950, (London: Chatto and Windus, 1991), p. 74.
5. *Ibid*, p. 72. (Note: The subsequent quoted words and phrases have been taken from the same book, page no. 72-73).
6. *Ibid*, p. 73.
7. *Ibid*, pp. 74-75.
8. *Ibid*, p. 75.
9. Desmond MacCarthy, Shaw, (London: Macgibbon and Kee, 1951), p. 163.
10. *Saint Joan*, Preface, p. 1.
11. *Saint Joan*, p. 67.
12. Arnold Silver, *Saint Joan: Playing With Fire*, (New York: Twayne Publishers, 1993), p. 44.
13. *Saint Joan*, p. 67.
14. *Ibid*, p. 68.
15. Arnold Silver, *Saint Joan: Playing With Fire*, p. 44.
16. *Saint Joan*, p. 124.
17. *Ibid*, pp. 10-11.

18. Michael Holroyd, *Bernard Shaw: The Lure of Fantasy*, Vol-III, 1918-1950, p. 77.
19. *Ibid*, p. 78.
20. Maurice Valency, *The Cart and the Trumpet: The Plays of George Bernard Shaw*, p. 375.
21. *Ibid.*
22. Desmond MacCarthy, *Shaw*, (London: Macgibbon and Kee, 1951), p. 166.
23. *Saint Joan*, Preface, p. 2.
24. *Saint Joan*, p. 123.
25. *Ibid*, p. 95.
26. *Ibid*, p. 90.
27. *Ibid*, p. 153.
28. *Saint Joan*, Preface, p. 33.
29. *Saint Joan*, p. 149.
30. Smith Warren Sylvester, "Bernard Shaw and the London Heretics," Seven Critical Essays, p. 65, as quoted in *George Bernard Shaw* - Vinod Bala Sharma, (New Delhi: Prestige Books, 1990), pp. 133-134.
31. Vinod Bala Sharma, *George Bernard Shaw*, (New Delhi: Prestige Books, 1990), p. 134.
32. *Saint Joan*, p. 75.
33. *Ibid*, pp. 106-107.
34. *Ibid*, p. 119.
35. *Ibid*, p. 139.
36. Michael Holroyd, Bernard Shaw: *The Lure of Fantasy*, Vol-III, 1918-1950, p. 77.
37. Maurice Valency, *The Cart and the Trumpet: The Plays of George Bernard Shaw*, pp. 378-379.
38. *Ibid.*
39. *Saint Joan*, Preface, p. 31
40. *Ibid.*
41. *Ibid*, pp. 11-12.
42. *Saint Joan*, p. 84.
43. Maurice Valency, *The Cart and the Trumpet: The Plays of George Bernard Shaw*, p. 383.

44. Michael Holroyd, *Bernard Shaw: The Lure of Fantasy*, Vol-III, 1918-1950, p. 78.
45. Arnold Silver, *Saint Joan: Playing With Fire*, p. 49.
46. *Saint Joan*, p. 101.
47. Arnold Silver, *Saint Joan: Playing With Fire*, p. 50.
48. *Ibid.*
49. *Saint Joan*, p. 128.
50. *Ibid*, p. 163.
51. Arnold Silver, *Saint Joan: Playing With Fire*, p. 53.
52. *Saint Joan*, Epilogue, p. 183.
53. Michael Holroyd, *Bernard Shaw: The Lure of Fantasy*, Vol-III, 1918-1950, p. 76.
54. *Saint Joan*, Epilogue, p. 180.
55. *Saint Joan*, p. 163.
56. Michael Holroyd, *Bernard Shaw: The Lure of Fantasy*, Vol-III, 1918-1950, p. 76.
57. *Ibid*, p. 78.
58. *Ibid*, p. 77.
59. *Ibid*, pp. 82-83.
60. Maurice Valency, *The Cart and the Trumpet: The Plays of George Bernard Shaw*, p. 379.
61. *Ibid*, p. 380.

6

Conclusion

After reading one of the plays of George Bernard Shaw, R.L. Stevenson made a comment to William Archer "I say, Archer, My God, what women!"[1] From Mrs. Warren, Major Barbara and Saint Joan, to Lina Szczepenowska the Polish acrobat-cum-Pilot of *Misalliance*—there is a formidable and awesome galaxy of new women, unwomanly women and boss women: they all justify Stevenson's exclamation. It goes to prove that Shaw was really "a first class ladies tailor" and the brilliant assemblage of women characters in his plays was aimed at highlighting and emphasizing the various female questions and problems which the society was not eager to recognise and to resolve. Known to the theatrical public as an *enfante terrible* Shaw's reputation grew as an iconoclast who created mischief in the theatre.

The present work has shown Shaw's unorthodox turn of mind and distrust of conventions and institutions as far as the status of women was concerned, both in the society as well as in the home. The preceding chapters of the thesis have clubbed the different types of women from the wide spectrum of Shavian panorama to form various categories. The emergence of the Shavian woman from Shaw's vision has kaleidoscopic characteristics: she is sometimes beyond our comprehension and sometimes a woman next door. She is the incarnation of Shaw's unorthodox frame of mind about the female; jealousy, the so-called womanish trait is not the feature of Shaw's woman. Her cool and composed maternal approach helps her get the desired man. Despite being voluptuous without vulgarity, she is a superwoman handling all the odds and ends—

from household chores to men. Illuminating this overall aspect Barbara Watson has written that she

> ...does her national housekeeping with relaxed efficiency, protects a man but never asks for protection, and is in all things a man's dream of perfection, may be impossible. She is made up of elements that already exist in living women and have existed through all the deprivations and deformities that male and female stupidity have combined to impose through the ages.[2]

Paradoxically, Shaw never made his woman rest on the pedestal of the superhumanly virtues of chastity, selflessness and other ideals. He set woman free of her image of paragon imposed upon her by her admirers cum exploiters. Shaw rationalised his ideal of equality between men and women and fished out the selfish motives behind the exaggeration of differences between men and women. He explored the idea that the obsession with chastity was an obsession with sex. The ulterior motive behind the ideal of the purity of women by keeping them out of business and politics was to lifeguard the laxity and debasement of the concerned fields. Shaw, by providing equality and freedom to woman in personal, professional and political spheres, projected her as the saviour of men's soul and the society.[3] This may be the reason why Shavian women "plunge into practical matters and change reality instead of shunning it."[4]

The Shavian woman, unlike other selfless women, is first and foremost, extremely "selfish." What Shaw means by being "selfish" is the "expression of self" which may be termed as "self-interest." This selfishness is the greatest virtue of the Shavian woman helping her to live her own life. In a society where men rule and predominate over everything, how will a woman survive without being self-assertive and self-assured? Extreme goodness, meaning self-denial, ruins itself and therefore only self-centred feelings can give her a genuine place, in the words of Watson:

> The selfishness Shaw recommends is extreme because only in its extreme form can it resist the insidious temptations of idealism, and...it [selfishness] in so many of the women in Shaw's plays becomes a saintly assurance and strength.[5]

In this way the selfishness Shaw recommends to woman means only honesty towards herself and her self-respect.

Another conspicuous characteristic of the Shavian woman is that she is the "aggressor in sex."[6] This unpleasant phrase has a pleasant connotation keeping in view Shaw's ideas about courtship, which he considers to be a game and not a war or a duel; therefore the Shavian huntress has been endowed with tact, wit and graceful charms with strong individualities. He used woman huntress as a stereotype to combat the Victorian stereotype of the Sexless Angel. Shaw, instead of making her timid womanly woman waiting to be wooed, makes her an independent wooer hunting for her suitor for the evolution of better generation. In the work of nature she explicitly makes her choice without being ashamed of it. Watson has written about this conception of woman that in the woman, who is a "vital genius," even

> ...unscrupulous or promiscuous behaviour is interpreted as the working of the evolutionary interpreted as the promptings of her unconscious self...a woman's pursuit of a lover need be no less the pursuit of an impersonal, evolutionary goal (a father for the superman) simply because it is inspired by sexual attraction.[7]

Since it can never be done consciously therefore the voice of the unconscious is necessary for it. If there would not be any attraction and charm, nobody would come to a woman only for procreation. In spite of being an initiator in conjugal relationship, a Shavian huntress does not have licentious relationship. There is no unwed mother or any immoral and lusty, love-ridden girl. She remains socially as well as personally conscious of what is good and respectable for her as well as for the society.

Shaw's theories about career women and their right to work for a living are also clear-cut and transparent. They are founded rationally on a desire for a sensibly arranged society. He recognised that the latent energy and ability of a woman could be used for the betterment of the world. Women's images must be equal or they will endeavour to drive the man's image down below subsistence level. Controlling and governing ability is so scarce that if competent women be ruled out, the places would be filled by reconciling incompetent and inefficient men. Shaw goes beyond the feminists demanding equal opportunity for work and writes that "If democracy were to mean equal consideration, then working mothers would have to be granted maternity leaves, maternity pensions and specially arranged working hours."[8] Shaw realises that a conscientious mother is sometimes a handicapped worker and he wants to put the burden of overcoming that handicap on the whole society instead of only on the individual woman. Shaw does something more valuable than demanding and asserting her right to equal treatment. He affirms her right to be a charming and feminine woman as well. "Feminity" in Shavian parlance is not akin to timidity and irresoluteness but indomitable will, physical and emotional strength, complacency, and physical attraction. The bossy and overbearing nature of women imparts them with a beauty of different kind. Shaw does not like the job of a secretary and he never created secretaries in his plays. Watson thinks that "one of Shaw's reasons for so insistently dramatizing their 'unwomanly' traits, including physical strength, is to emphasize as strongly as possible their charm, their feminity, and the final, unanswerable evidence of their imperial success in love."[9]

Shaw's reflections on sexual equality form a complex legacy mixing the ideas he formulated as a political thinker and as a socialist. Some critics believe that the portrayals of women in his plays are disparaging while others see them as the prototype of emancipated women. According to Michael Holroyd "the trouble with Bernard Shaw is that we always believe what he says. Whether the topic is war, wool, or women, his assertions strike with the force of commandments."[10]

Viewed traditionally Shaw's contribution is positive. The strong, dynamic, independent women of the plays were regarded as the prime source of inspiration for the Victorian women to break the shackles of traditional upbringing and both Shaw and the women were dependent upon each other for mutual need and appreciation. As Wilma Meikle recorded in 1915 that young women at the universities, held Shaw's work in high esteem and simply "poured over" them. Wells adjudged that these were the real guides to the emancipation of women.[11] Lady Rhondda set down that

Shaw's generalisations on these matters require observation because the intelligentsia take him seriously on women issues.[12] In spite of all audacious Shavian discussions, there is no character who infringes the conventions in practice. He never brought anarchic thing as an unmarried mother on to his stage. Gareth Griffith explored the reason behind it that Shaw always took the middle course mixing revolution with morality and therefore "fundamental to his many roles was that of a moral revolutionary."[13] As a "moral revolutionary" Shaw portrayed his women figures for whom moral passion was the real passion.

Shaw's relationships with women in his personal life were very complex and complicated. Explaining this mind boggling association with women Gareth Griffith has written that:

> Personally Shaw's relationships with women were extremely odd, a combination of fascination and wariness, candour and evasive charm, a curious mixture of lover and sprite, the emotional tease who made women fall for him only to toy with their affections, sending them on their way but with an armful of witty letters for company.[14]

Shaw's relationship with his mother, Lucinda, was not in general a mother-son attachment: she was cool, hard, aggressive and rational. Shaw rejected his father and desired to identify with his mother, an identification made possible by her "masculinity." This encouraged Shaw to develop traditionally feminine characteristics like physical modesty, narcissism, vanity, flirtatiousness, charm and talkativeness; at the same time he rejected the war-sport-women. But unfortunately Shaw's mother did not return his sympathy and this made Shaw comment somewhere that she did not hate nor love anybody. Thus her coldness towards Shaw made him feel insecure where women were concerned and also in awe of their powers. H.C. Duffin has written that Shaw's consideration of his women helps to conclude that he had developed certain female characteristics and that "Orinthia may be taken as speaking for Shaw when she says to Magnus, 'you are less of a fool and less of a moral coward than any man I have ever known. You have almost the makings of a first rate woman in you'."[15]

The absence of maternal love and filial affection made him experience "emotional isolation in childhood [and he] sought and thrived on women's affections but drew back from committing his own."[16] His amatory liaison with a number of beautiful, intelligent women and actresses like Florence Farr, Ellen Terry, Janet Achurch, Mrs Patrick Campbell, Molly Tompkins, Annie Besant, May Morris flourished but ended in smoke. But Shaw utilized his experiences with different women of substance and framed his women figures in his plays on them. Shaw abhorred sex, adopted harsh attitude towards possessive women in his emotional affairs yet, Shaw, "the realist, the destroyer of the illusions of romantic love, was himself under the spell of the romantic fascination of women."[17] His platonic married life supported him more than anything else. Shaw expressed to Alexandra Kropotkin that he inspired young people because Charlotte managed his life so much so that he could get leisure time to work and to call on friends. Without Charlotte he could not have come out with flying colours.[18]

Many a women and critics have condemned Shaw and regarded him as an exploiter who capitalized on women's emotions to get material for the "writing machine" G.B.S. and that Shaw's dried, emotionless, affinity with women gets reflection in his cold, sexless, emotionless women characters in his plays. Catling quoted that "Shaw was a pioneer feminist who exploited women."[19] Edith Nesbit, a poet and a novelist, was also infatuated with Shaw. She wrote about Shaw:

> He is a very clever writer and speaker—is the grossest flatterer (of men, women and children impartially) I ever met, is horribly untrustworthy...does not always stick to the truth...is one of the most fascinating men I ever met. Everyone rather affects to despise him...but everyone admires him all the same. Miss Hoatson pretends to hate him, but my impression is that she is over head and ears in love with him.[20]

Ellen Terry, who acted Lady Cicely, gave an account of him "He is not a man of convictions: That is one of the charms of his plays—to me at least. One never knows how the cat is really jumping. But it jumps. Bernard Shaw is alive, with nine lives, like that cat!"[21]

Bertha Newcombe, a Fabian and a professional artist, who was supposed to get married to Shaw, wrote that Shaw was a "passionless man" with

> ...no wish for and even to fear passion though he admitted its power and pleasure. The sight of a woman deeply in love with him annoyed him...he had decided...a line of honourable conduct—honourable to his thinking...while allowing himself every opportunity of transgressing the spirit. Frequent talking, talking, talking of the pros and cons of marriage...his dislike of the sexual relation and so on, would create an atmosphere of love-making without any need for caresses or endearments.[22]

She upheld that "Shaw has not a gift of sympathetic penetration into a woman's nature. He employs his clever detective power and pounces on weaknesses and faults which confirm his pre-conceived ideas."[23] Beatrice Webb was a keen observer of Shaw's nature and observed that this "brilliant philanderer"

> ...idealises them [women] for a few days, weeks or years, imagines them to be something utterly different from their true selves, then has a revulsion of feeling and discovers them to be unutterably vulgar, second rate, rapscallion, or insipidly well-bred.... In fact it is not the end he caves for; it is the process.[24]

Thus he simply got "delight in being the candle to the moths, with a dash of intellectual curiosity to give flavour to his tickled vanity."[25] Alexandra Kropotkin quoted that it always seemed to him that the "intricacies of the female mind...female character were beyond his understanding.... He, the great master, of malice, simply couldn't understand this feminine twist."[26]

These are the observations and comments of some of the important persons in Shaw's social circle. On an astute observation of these few reflections it can be figured out that Shaw's relationships with women had different shades. These opinions portray Shaw's role as an onlooker, reporter and a creative writer. First he watched women, then as a reporter "turned everything inside out to see whether the other side won't do just as well if not better; it is this fanaticism which gives him genuine charm."[27] After analysing, as a creative writer he moulded his women characters in the somewhat same moral, mental shape taking help of his realistic and idealistic vision.

Some more perceptions of the women who were concerned with Shaw's personal life reveal many aspects of his personality. Charlotte, Shaw's soul mate, revealed that Bernard Shaw

> ...is a man the direct opposite of what the world thinks...he is an atheist, a vegetarian, a firm believer in women's rights, going so far as to espouse the feminist movement...he has been a vegetarian for thirty years, because he does not believe in the killing of animals.[28]

She thought that he was a through feminist who wanted women to be placed on all governing boards.[29] What she meant to say was that a great man, a dreamer of wonderful dreams, an idealist and an individualist who always strived to lift others to the high plane of his own thought and beliefs was "bashful and refining, quiet and reserved by value" but he never "let this part of his nature overrule him."[30] Annie Besant's impression of Shaw was as

> ...one of the most brilliant of socialist writers and most provoking of men...with a passion for representing himself as a scoundrel...he was a writer with principles and preferred starving his body to starving his conscience...[31]

Mrs. Patrick Campbell, a formidable actress, posed the most serious threat to Shaw's marriage that it was ever to face. In her words:

> There was one who perhaps through the intelligent grasp of his genius, understood a little the nerve rack of my illness. Himself living in dreams, he made a dream-world for me. Only those who can understand this can understand the friendship Bernard Shaw gave to me by my sickbed...I have sometimes thought that perhaps it is only human heart he hides and fears.[32]

Lawrence Langner, theatre director, founder of the Theatre Guild, observed the Shaws and said that Mrs. Shaw lovingly called Shaw "the Genius" who was "guided by her excellent common sense, which often served as an antidote to his tendency to explode fireworks on all occasions."[33] Mrs. Margaret Smith, "Maggie"—Shaw's parlourmaid for the last sixteen years of his life wrote "Mr. Shaw had no violent dislikes for anybody. I don't think Mr. Shaw would do anybody a wrong turn, even if he wouldn't do them a good one... 'Give them an inch and they take a mile,' were the only sort of people Mr. Shaw didn't like."[34] Mrs. Jisbella Lyth, the legendary village post-mistress of Ayot St. Lawrence reminisced that "Mr Shaw was years ahead of his time..."[35] She expressed that "some said Mr. Shaw was a humbug; but aren't we all? Shaw was straight if ever a man was.... Others had perhaps only one thing in their lives—Shaw had many things."[36] It can be concluded, having examined all these reminiscences, that Shaw combined his "artistic nature, his genius...with being an ordinary man...."[37]

We should bear these complicating, contradictory personal factors in mind while discussing Shaw's views about women and sexual equality because "the connection between private experience and public utterance is especially intense."[38] Shaw never regarded women as animals of another species and had no difficulty, as a playwright, in creating female dramatis personae as easily and adroitly as male ones. His radical feminist view was that human nature is neither exclusively masculine nor feminine but a combination of the both with "the perceived attributes of womanliness and manliness owing more to the preserves of environment and convention than to any natural, deep-seated traits of personality."[39] He always assumed that a woman is a person exactly like himself. On the proposal of the actress Margaret Halston to "ghost write" a short speech for her on "The women in Shaw's Plays" he revealed that there was no woman in his plays. Thus Margaret Halston came to the conclusion that the reason the women in his plays were so uncommonly good is that he always assumes that a "woman is just like a man" but men were "slightly more hysterical" than women because of "being cuddled by women from their childhood."[40] It does not mean that Shaw negated feminity but believed in an androgynous nature of personality. The vogue of women copying masculine dresses and vile habits such as smoking, drinking, slapping, abusing, was a prevalent trend in the late nineteenth century. Shaw propounded that masculine affectations were always a mistake and by imitating manly conduct women were enslaving themselves. He suggested that women should assert the social value of being women by demonstrating their sufficiency and insufficiency of masculinity. Thus if we take Shaw's views about women constructively it can be concluded that, "the defining features of his radical feminism were the substitution of equality for hierarchy together with an emphasis on similarity instead of difference."[41] If we take it critically it is apparently clear that it "undermine[s] the Victorian ideal of the self-sacrificing womanly woman."[42] Basic to Shaw's feminism was the advocacy for moral, physical and social emancipation of women with dignity and self-respect for every individual woman, which would transform the family relationships contributing to the evolution of a new society.

For Shaw drama was a vehicle for expressing his provocative views in the form of entertainment. This was the mode he used to put forth his suggestions of the true way in which to view human experience and institutions. If he appears to be satirical his satire is aimed at the audience and not at his creations on the stage. He says, "I must warn my readers that my attacks are directed against themselves, not against my stage figures."[43]

Being a dramatic critic for many years he had the expertise to mould the dramatic form to suit his needs. He took the accepted pattern of Victorian melodrama or farce or drawing room comedy and, at the most effective moments, inverted it, as it were, transposing the parts of the conventional hero and the conventional villain; and then, having done that and having led his audience to believe that this is a revolutionary or iconoclastic play, he inverts it again, and shows that the conventional hero is, after all, a hero but in a new sense. This double inversion is an immensely successful dramatic device, but it is more than that: it is part of Shaw's technique for making his audience look again and again at the particular situation he is presenting, until they have shed all illusions bred either by convention or by facile anti-conventionality.

It was due to Shaw's puritanism that he could not easily combine the intellect and the body in his fictional women characters. Hence his female protagonists are endowed more with intellect than with sex appeal. These women in Shaw's plays have provoked the critics down the years to pass judgement either in their favour or against them. One argument against these characters has been that they are untrue to life, invented merely for the stage, "born out of a union between Ibsen and Shaw in their well publicized elopement from Victorian sentiment."[44] Susanne Langer's theory of "Dramatic Illusion" can be taken into consideration for understanding why Shaw's characters appeared "untrue to life" in his age. The critic's argument is that literature projects an image of life "in the mode of virtual memory" through language. The depiction is of life as lived in the past. But "Dramatic Illusion" is different from this kind of representation:

> ...drama presents the poetic illusion in a different light: not finished realities, or 'events,' but immediate, visible responses of human beings, makes its semblance of life. Its basic abstraction is the act, which springs from past, but is directed toward the future, and is always great with things to come.[45]

Shaw's characterisation of Lilith in *Back to Methuselah* bears testimony to this theoretical assessment. Lilith is the one in whom father and mother are one. She says:

> Of life only is there no end; and though of its million starry mansions many are empty and many still unbuilt, and though its vast domain is as yet unbearably desert, my seed shall one day fill it and master its matter to its uttermost confines.[46]

These last words of hers hint at male and female being one. Shaw appreciated Hinduism because it advocates the idea of modern feminism by making Shiva a woman as well as a man.[47] Shaw always attempted to get freedom from the confines of the natural world, which was one of senses. Subsequently he desired freedom from natural life. The theme of *Back to Methuselah* is "not longevity as an idea itself, but longevity as a means of transcending the present period of short aims and disbelief in the future. So far as it is possible to the vision of the future into a play, Shaw, perhaps does it."[48] Perhaps his exposition appears to be unsatisfactory, but this could be because the future is not known to his audience and hence cannot be expressed in words.

Therefore while Shaw's contemporaries were creating heroines who were more and more womanly, Shaw was engrossed in creating women who were just like men as they would prove to be in the next century though they may be termed as "unsexed women." Shaw created women in the interest of political egalitarianism because he thought that a "man is a woman without petticoats." In his fight for equality he preferred women to govern in the interest of "national housekeeping," because he thought that women were the same as men but different, and perhaps were a fractionless idiotic than them.

REFERENCES

1. Michael Holroyd, ed. *The Genius of Shaw: A Symposium*, (London: Hodder and Stoughton, George Rainbird Ltd., 1979), p. 167.
2. Barbara Bellow Watson, *A Shavian Guide to The Intelligent Woman*, (London: Chatto and Windus, 1964), p. 204.
3. *Ibid*, p. 205.
4. *Ibid*.
5. *Ibid*.
6. Michael Holroyd, ed. *The Genius of Shaw: A Symposium*, p. 205.
7. Barbara Bellow Watson, *A Shavian Guide to The Intelligent Woman*, p. 205.
8. *Ibid*, p. 210.
9. *Ibid*.
10. Michael Holroyd, *The Genius of Shaw*, p. 185.
11. W. Miekle, *Towards a Sane Feminism*, (London: Grant Richards, 87) as quoted in *Socialism and Superior Brains*: The Political Thought of Bernard Shaw, Gareth Griffith, (London: Routledge, 1993), p. 57.
12. Lady Rhondda (1930a), 'Shaw's Women,' *Time and Tide*, 7 March: 300-1, as quoted in *Socialism and Superior Brains*: The Political Thought of Bernard Shaw, Gareth Griffith, (London: Routledge, 1993), pp. 157-158.
13. Gareth Griffith, *Socialism and Superior Brains: The Political Thought of Bernard Shaw*, (London: Routledge, 1993), p. 301.

14. *Ibid*, p. 160.
15. H.C. Duffin, *The Quintessence of Bernard Shaw*, (New Delhi: General Book Depot, 1939), p. 46.
16. A.M. Gibbs, ed., *Shaw: Interviews and Recollections*, (Iowa City: University of Iowa Press, 1990), p. 159.
17. Gareth Griffith, *Socialism and Superior Brains: The Political Thought of Bernard Shaw*, p. 160.
18. A.M. Gibbs, ed., *Shaw: Interviews and Recollections*, p. 159.
19. P.S. Catling, (1981), "Love by Letter" *Sunday Telegraph*, 12 April: 256 as quoted in *Socialism and Superior Brains: The Political Thought of Bernard Shaw*, Gareth Griffith, (London: Routledge, 1993), p. 158.
20. A.M. Gibbs, ed., *Shaw: Interviews and Recollections*, p. 162.
21. *Ibid*, p. 163.
22. *Ibid*, p. 167.
23. *Ibid*.
24. *Ibid*, p. 169.
25. *Ibid*.
26. *Ibid*, p. 179.
27. *Ibid*, p. 170.
28. *Ibid*, p. 180.
29. *Ibid*.
30. *Ibid*.
31. *Ibid*, p. 161.
32. *Ibid*, p. 175.
33. *Ibid*, p. 181.
34. Allan Chappelow, ed., *Shaw: The Villager and Human Being—A Biographical Symposium*, (London: Charles Skilton Ltd. 1961), p. 48.
35. *Ibid*, p. 83.
36. *Ibid*, p. 89.
37. *Ibid*, p. 91.
38. Gareth Griffith, *Socialism and Superior Brains: The Political Thought of Bernard Shaw*, p. 161.
39. *Ibid*, p. 162.
40. D.H. Lawrence, ed., *Shaw: Collected Letters 1911-1925*, (London: Max Reinhardt, 1985b) as quoted in Gareth Griffith, *Socialism and Superior Brains: The Political Thought of Bernard Shaw*, p. 162.

41. Gareth Griffith, *Socialism and Superior Brains: The Political Thought of Bernard Shaw*, p. 162.
42. *Ibid*, p. 162.
43. As Quoted in David Daiches, *A Critical History of English Literature*, Vol. 4, Allied Publishers, New Delhi, 1983, p. 1104.
44. Michael Holroyd, ed. *The Genius of Shaw: A Symposium*, p. 170.
45. Susanne K. Langer, *Feeling and Form: A Theory of Art Developed from Philosophy in a New Key*, (London: Routledge and Kegan Paul Ltd., 1967), p. 306.
46. C.B. Purdom, *A Guide to the Plays of Bernard Shaw*, (London: Methuen, 1963), p. 270.
47. Dan H. Laurence, *Bernard Shaw: Collected Letters 1926-1950*, Vol. 4, (London: Max Reinhardt, 1988), p. 322.
48. C.B. Purdom, *A Guide to the Plays of Bernard Shaw*, p. 270.

Bibliography

Primary Sources

Shaw, George Bernard. *The Intelligent Woman's Guide to Socialism, Capitalism, Sovietism And Fascism*, Vol. I, Great Britain: Penguin Books Limited, 1937.

——. *The Quintessence of Ibsenism*, London: Constable & Co., 1913.

——. *The Complete Prefaces of Bernard Shaw*, London: Paul Hamlyn Ltd., 1965.

——. *Major Barbara*, ed. S. Sengupta, Delhi: Surjeet Publications, 1979.

——. *Pygmalion*, ed. S. Sengupta, Delhi: Surjeet Publications, 1985.

——. *Saint Joan*, ed. A.C. Ward, Hyderabad: Orient Longman Ltd., 1995.

——. *Man and Superman*, ed. S. Sengupta, Delhi: Surjeet Publications, 2000.

——. *Candida*, ed. S. Sengupta, Delhi: Surjeet Publications, 1980.

——. *Arms And The Man*, ed. A.C. Ward Hyderabad: Orient Longman, 1983.

——. *The Philanderer, Complete Plays with Prefaces* Vol. I-VI, New York: Dodd, Mead & Company, 1962.

——. *Mrs. Warren's Profession, Complete Plays with Prefaces* Vol. I-VI, New York: Dodd, Mead & Company, 1962.

——. *Misalliance, Complete Plays with Prefaces* Vol. I-VI, New York: Dodd, Mead & Company, 1962.

——. *Collected Letters 1926-1950*, Vol. 4, ed. Dan H. Laurence, New York: Max Reinhardt, 1988.

Secondary Sources

Archer, William. *The Old Drama And The New: An Essay In Re-valuation*. London: William Heinemann Ltd., 1923.

Abraham, Taisha ed., *Feminist Theory And Modern Drama*. Delhi: Pencraft International, 1998.

Beauvoir, Simone De. *The Second Sex*, ed. and trans. H.M. Parshley, London: Vintage, 1997.

Booth, Michael R. *Prefaces to English Nineteenth Century Theatre*, London: Manchester University Press, 1988.

Brustin, Robert. *The Theatre of Revolt*, London: Methuen and Co. Ltd., 1965.

Crompton, Louis. *Shaw the Dramatist: A Study of the Intellectual Background of the Major Plays*, London: George Allen and Unwin Ltd, 1971.

Cohn, Ruby. *Currents in Contemporary Drama*, London: Indiana University Press, 1969.

Corrigan, Robert W. *The Modern Theatre*, New York: The Macmillan Company, 1966.

Chesterton, G.K. *George Bernard Shaw*, New Delhi: Atlantic Publishers and Distributors, 1990.

Cann, C. G.L. Du. *The Loves of George Bernard Shaw*, London: Arthur Barker Limited, 1963.

Chappelow, Allan. ed., *Shaw The Villager And Human Being: A Biographical Symposium*, London: Charles Skilton Ltd., 1961.

Duffin, H.C. *The Quintessence of Bernard Shaw*, Delhi: General Book Depot, 1939.

Eagleton, Mary. *Feminist Literary Criticism*, London: Longman, 1991.

Evans, T.F. ed., *Shaw: The Critical Heritage*, London: Routledge and Kegan Paul, 1976.

Finney, Gail. *Women in Modern Drama: Freud, Feminism and European Theatre at the Turn of the Century*, London: Cornell University Press, 1989.

Gupta, S.C. Sen. *The Art of Bernard Shaw*, Calcutta: A. Mukherjee and Co, Pvt. Ltd., 1957.

Gibbs, A.M. ed., *Shaw: Interviews and Recollections*, Iowa City: University of Iowa Press, 1990.

Gibbs, A.M. *The Art and Mind of Shaw: Essays in Criticism*, London: The Macmillan Press Ltd, 1983.

Griffith, Gareth. *Socialism and Superior Brains: The Political Thought of Bernard Shaw*, London: Routledge, 1993.

Gainer, J. Ellen. *Shaw's Daughters: Dramatic and Narrative Constructions of Gender*, Ann Arbar: University of Michigan Press, 1991.

Harris, Frank. *Bernard Shaw: An Unauthorised Biography based on first hand information with a postscript by Shaw*, New York: Simon and Schuster, 1931.

Hugo, Leon. *Bernard Shaw: Playwright and Preacher*, London: Methuen and Co. Ltd., 1971.

Hunt, Hugh, Kenneth Richards & John Ruesell Taylor. *The Revels History of Drama in English*, Vol. VII, 1880 to the Present Day, London: Methuen and Co. Ltd., 1978.

Holroyd, Michael. *Bernard Shaw: The Pursuit of Power*, Vol. II, 1898-1918, London: Chatto and Windus, 1989.

Holroyd, Michael. *Bernard Shaw, The Search for Love*, Vol. I, 1866-1898, London: Chatto and Windus, 1988.

Holroyd, Michael. *Bernard Shaw, The Lure of Fantasy*, Vol. III, 1918-1950, London: Chatto and Windus, 1991.

Holledge, Julie. *Innocent Flowers: Women in the Edwardian Theatre*, London: Virago, 1981.

Innes, Christopher. *Modern British Drama 1890-1990*, Cambridge: Cambridge University Press, 1992.

Jalote, S.R. *Shaw's Principles of Literary Criticism*, Varanasi: Rishi Publications, 1987.

Kaplan, Cora. *Sea Changes: Essays on Culture and Feminism*, London; Verso, 1986.

Kaufmann, R.J. ed., *G.B. Shaw: A Collection of Critical Essays*, New Jersey: Prentice-Hall, 1965.

Kaye, Julian B. *Bernard Shaw and the Nineteenth Century Tradition*, U.S.A., Norman: University of Oklahoma Press, 1958.

MacCarthy, Desmond. *Shaw*, London: Macgibbon and Kee, 1951.

Meyer, Michael. comp. *IBSEN on File*, London: Methuen, 1985.

Morgan, Margery M. *The Shavian Playground: An Exploration of the Art of George Bernard Shaw*, London: Methuen and Co. Ltd., 1974.

Millet, Kate. *Sexual Politics*, New York: Doubleday and Company, 1970.

Nicoll, Allardyce. *English Drama 1900-1930: The Beginnings of the Modern Period*, Cambridge: Cambridge University Press, 1973.

Pearson, Hesketh. *Bernard Shaw: His Life and Personality*, London: Methuen and Co. Ltd., 1961.

Purdom, C.B. *A Guide to the Plays of Bernard Shaw*, London: Methuen, 1963.

Sushila Singh ed., *Recent Trends in Feminist Thought*, New Delhi: Prestige Books, 1991.

Silver, Arnold. *Saint Joan: Playing with Fine*, New York: Twayne Publishers, 1993.

Showalter, Elaine. *A Literature of Their Own: British Women Novelists From Bronte to Lessing*. New Jersey: Princeton University Press, 1977.

Showalter, Elaine ed., *Women's Liberation and Literature*, New York: Harcourt Brace Jovanovich, Inc., 1971.

Showalter, Elaine. *Speaking of Gender*, New York: Routledge, 1989.

Sodhi, Meena. *Shaw's Candida: A Critical Appreciation*, New Delhi: Atlantic Publishers and Distributors, 1995.

Sharma, Vinod Bala. *George Bernard Shaw*, New Delhi: Prestige Books, 1990.

Sagan, Eli. *Freud, Women And Morality: The Psychology of Good and Evil*. New York: Basic Books, Inc., 1988.

Taylor, John Russell. *The Rise and Fall of The Well Made Play*, London: Methuen and Co. Ltd., 1967.

Valency, Maurice. *The Cart And The Trumpet: The Plays of George Bernard Shaw*, New York: Oxford University Press, 1973.

Williams, Raymond. *DRAMA: From Ibsen to Brecht*, London: Chatto and Windus, 1971.

Wisenthal, J.L. *The Marriage of Contraries: Bernard Shaw's Middle Plays*, Cambridge: Harvard University Press, 1974.

Weedon, Chris. *Feminist Practice and Poststructuralist Theory*, UK: Blackwell Publishers Ltd., 1987.

Lyon, Mary, ed. *Virginia Woolf: Books and Portraits*, London: The Hogarth Press, 1977.

Watson, Barbara Bellow. *A Shavian Guide to the Intelligent Woman*, London: Chatto and Windus, 1964.

Greene, Nicholas. *Bernard Shaw: A Critical View*, New York: St. Martin's Press, 1984.

Sodhi, Meena. *Indian English Writing: The Autobiographical Mode*, New Delhi: Creative Books, 1999.

Langer, Susanne K. *Feeling and Form: A Theory of Art Developed From Philosophy in a New Key*, London: Routledge and Kegan Paul Limited, 1967.

Thesis Works

Sharma, Niti. *Feminism in Contemporary British and Indian Fiction in English*, 1994, Department of English, B.H.U.

Sinha, Sunanda Kr. *Fiction of Ruth Pawar Jhabvala: A Feminist Perspective*, 1995, Department of English, B.H.U.

Encyclopaedia

Gassner, John and Edward Quinne ed., *The Encyclopaedia of World Drama*, London: Methuen and Co. Ltd., 1970.

McGraw-Hill Encyclopaedia of World Drama, An International Reference Work in four volumes, New York: Mcgraw Hill Book Co., 1972.

The New Encyclopaedia Britannia v. 12, Micropedia Ready Reference, 15th Ed, Chicago: Encyclopaedia Britannia, 1985.

Articles

Dukore, Bernard F. "The Fabian and the Freudian." *The Shavian* 4th Ser. 2 (June 1961): 8-11.

Batson, Eric J. "Mr. Bernard Shaw and Ladies." *The Shavian* 4th Ser. 2 (June 1961): 23-27.

Mason, Ronald. "A Speech On Shaw." *The Shavian* 18th Ser. 3 (Winter, 1968-1969): 13-16.

Kornbluth, Martin L. "Two Fallen Women: Paula Tanqueray and Kitty Warren." *The Shavian* 14th Ser (Feb. 1959): 14-15.

Cole, John. "Bernard Shaw - The Patient." *The Shavian* 7th Ser. 7 (Spring, 1995): 12.

Sagittarius. "An Intelligent Woman Guiding the Shavians." *The Shavian* 7th, 8th Ser. 4 (Summer, 1973): 145-249.

Lorichs, Sonja. "The Unwomanly Woman." *The Shavian* 7th, 8th Ser. 4 (Summer, 1973): 250-252.

Khanna, Savitri. "Shaw's Image of Woman." *The Shavian* 7th, 8th Ser. 4 (Summer, 1973): 253-259.

Gorlin, Vernon. "Bernard Shaw and Three 'Dark Ladies'." *The Shavian* Vol. 3, No. 5 (Summer, 1966): 23-26.

Crawford, Fred D. "Shaw's British Inheritors." *The Shavian* Vol. 7, No. 1 (Spring, 1991): 12-16.

Tresize, Simon. "The Intelligent Person's Guide To Shaw's Comic Art." *The Shavian* Vol. 7, No. 3 (Summer, 1992): 10-14.

Evans, Judith. "Shaw's Fabian Tracts And His Political Plays." *The Shavian* Vol. 7, No. 3 (Summer, 1992): 15-21.

Weintraub, Stanley. "Caesar and Cleopatra: A Melbourne: Victoria dimension." *The Shavian* Vol. 6, No. 6 (Spring, 1988): 6-8.

Ravindranathan, S. "The Life Force in the Offing: A reinterpretation of Widowers' Houses." *The Shavian* Vol. 7, No. 3 (Summer, 1992): 9-11.

Mudford, Peter. "Mrs. Warren's Profession." *The Shavian* 6th Ser. 6 (Spring, 1987): 4-10.

Dench, Judi. "Barbara and I." *The Shavian* 4th Ser. 4 (Spring, 1971): 120-122.

Nethercot, Arthur H. "The Vivie-Frank Relationship in Mrs. Warren's Profession." *The Shavian* 15th Ser. (June, 1959): 7-9.

Weintraub, Stanley. "Bernard Shaw's Other Saint Joan" *The Shavian* 18th Ser. 2 (Oct. 1964): 7-13.

Worth, Katharine J. "Shaw and John Osborne.' *The Shavian* 18th Ser. 2 (Oct. 1964): 29-35.

Vaid, Sudesh. "Ideologies on Women in Nineteenth Century Britain, 1850s-70s." Review of Women Studies (October, 1985) *Economic And Political Weekly*, WS63-WS67.

Denison, Patricia D. "Victorian and Modern Drama: Social Convention and Theatrical Invention in T.W. Robertson's Plays." *Modern Drama*, 37 (1994), 401-420.

Forrey, Carolyn. "The New Woman Revisited," *Women's Studies*, 2 (1974), 38.

Stein, Kate Trimble. "The Art of Selection," *Club Women*, (December 1897), 76.

Index

A

B

C

D

E

F

G

H